THE
BLACK WIDOW
SPIDER

Raymond W. Thorp and
Weldon D. Woodson

With a Foreword by
Emil Bogen

Dover Publications, Inc.
New York

Published in Canada by General Publishing
Company, Ltd., 30 Lesmill Road, Don Mills,
Toronto, Ontario.
Published in the United Kingdom by Constable
and Company, Ltd., 10 Orange Street, London
WC2H 7EG.

This Dover edition, first published in 1976, is
an unabridged republication of the work originally
titled *Black Widow; America's Most Poisonous
Spider* and published by the University of North
Carolina Press, Chapel Hill, in 1945.

International Standard Book Number: 0-486-23405-3
Library of Congress Catalog Card Number: 76-23978

Manufactured in the United States of America
Dover Publications, Inc.
180 Varick Street
New York, N.Y. 10014

Acknowledgments

wwwwwwwwwwwwwwwwwwwwwwwwwwwwwwwwwwwwwwwwwwwwwwwwwwwwwwwwwwwwwwww

THIS book is based upon the findings of students of spider bites from ancient to contemporary times, and upon the authors' personal investigations. We feel a deep gratitude to all contributors listed in the bibliography, and wish to express our appreciation for the courteous co-operation of the Los Angeles County Medical Association Library, the Army Medical Library in Washington, D. C., and the Los Angeles Public Library. In our investigations we are indebted to Charles Barton, M. D., Assistant City Health Officer of Los Angeles, for technical data; Bernard Schoenberg for assistance in translating the foreign literature; Keith Boyd, Newton Berlin, Leo. G. Young, W. B. Herms, Wayne Book, and the U. S. Department of Agriculture for aid in the preparation of the illustrations; Carroll Thorp for his field work in collecting arachnids for observation purposes; various laymen (victims of black widow spider bites) for their replies to our questionnaire; and scores of physicians, registered nurses, and lay heads of hospitals and other institutions for their communications concerning black widow spider-bite pa-

tients. The greatest contribution, however, was furnished
by Emil Bogen, M. D., whose knowledge in this special
field is probably not exceeded by that of any other man.

Material used in Chapter VIII is from Dr. Bogen's
articles as follows: "Arachnidism: A Study in Spider Poisoning," *Journal of the American Medical Association*
(June 19, 1926); "Poisonous Spider Bites, Newer Developments in our Knowledge of Arachnidism," *Annals of
Internal Medicine* (September, 1932); "Poisoning Poisonous Spiders" (By Emil Bogen and Russell N. Loomis),
California and Western Medicine (July, 1936). For permission to quote from these articles, we wish to thank Dr.
Bogen and the editors of the journals.

RAYMOND W. THORP
WELDON D. WOODSON

Los Angeles, California

Foreword

~~~~~~

THE struggle for survival between man and his natural enemies throughout the ages—the wolf, the worm, the germ and the virus—favors the best adapted rather than the most offensive and best armored forms. Natural history is not only a most interesting and absorbing pastime, but is indeed one of the means by which man learns to adapt himself to his environment—and to achieve supremacy.

Spiders may indeed be useful and inoffensive allies of man when they confine their efforts to the entrapment of the typhoid fly and the adornment of lawns and rosebushes; but the particular species which forms the subject of this book is no neutral bystander or friendly neighbor. Hundreds of deaths and thousands of sufferers prove her vicious character.

The authors of this book have not attempted an exhaustive scientific treatise on all aspects of the Arachnida. On the other hand, by amassing a wealth of citations and observations they have presented convincing evidence of the character of the black widow spider, and set forth practically all that is known concerning this ferocious enemy of mankind for the edification of professional as well as laymen. The times this manuscript has been re-written, with the great labor which such painstaking work entails, can be appreciated only by one who has seen it grow.

This is not the last word that will be said on the subject of the black widow spider. Such a widespread and ferocious form cannot but continue to add interesting chapters to its guerilla-warfare history. It is, however, an extensive review of all that has gone before, and may well serve as a point of departure for future studies.

EMIL   BOGEN,   M.D.

Olive View, California

Contents

∿∿∿

Illustrations

~~~~~~

THE
BLACK WIDOW
SPIDER

1. Spider Lore and Legend

wwwwwwwwwwwwwwwwwwwwwwwwwwwwwwwwwwwwwwwwwwwwwwwwwwwwwwwwwwwwwwwwwwww

SPIDERS and spider bites have received the attention of mankind since the days of the ancients. Many brilliant minds have speculated upon the ways of the creatures, and not a few have voiced opinions concerning their poison propensities. Humankind in the mass have noted their daily habits, and imagination has given birth to numerous traditions and legends. Every age and every clime has had its wealth of imaginative lore.

In Hebrew Biblical history there are two accepted references to the spider, and according to some translations, it is mentioned several other times. The two Bible references are found in Job and Isaiah, where both writers use the spider's web as an emblem of frailty. The first declares that the "trust" of the ungodly shall be equivalent to that of a spider's web; and the second, in reproaching the human transgressors of that time, uses various expressions, not the least of which is that "they weave the spider's web." There is also the apocryphal story of King David and the spider, which reveals a friendly disposition toward the creature.

In the legendary history of the Greeks there is the story of the origin of the name Arachnida. Told at length by the Roman poet, Ovid, in his *Metamorphoses*, it formed the basis for Spenser's mention in his *Muiopoto-mos* and for many other paraphrases throughout the prose and poetry of the world. Arachne, a beautiful girl highly skilled in weaving, once challenged Athene (Minerva), goddess of the distaff, to a contest. Arachne wove a tapestry of marvellous beauty on which she depicted the amours of the gods and goddesses. The beauty and the subject of the tapestry so enraged the goddess that she destroyed the web. Arachne, overcome with despair, hanged herself, whereupon Athene changed her into a spider.

The Chinese, according to Ball, look upon the spider with favor, at times even with awe. Their fauna includes scores of species of spiders, some with bodies as large as small birds, which spin their webs from tree to tree high up in the air. A portion of the folklore pertains to these mammoth spiders, and other tales tell of spiders in general, emphasizing in particular their webs. Werner cites a narrative that concerns Sun Houtzu, the Monkey Fairy, who became a god. Once he encountered the Sisters who transformed themselves into huge spiders, and were able to spin ropes instead of webs with which to bind their enemies. However, Sun was able to attack and kill them.

Pliny, in his writings, portrayed the spider as a ferocious creature and noted that she was most dangerous during the summer. In one of his references the "venomous bite" of the creature is recorded, while in another, he describes the procedure used by a spider to subdue a snake. The spider is poised in her web in a tree while the snake lies coiled in the shade beneath. From her aerial position the spider launches an attack by throwing herself upon the head of the reptile and piercing its brain with her fangs. "Such is the shock," he relates, "that the creature will hiss from time to time, and then seized with vertigo, coil round and round, while it finds itself unable to take flight, or so much as break the web of the spider. . . . This scene only ends with its death."

Strabo, who wrote during the first century, quotes Diodorus Siculus as recording a plague of spiders which had far-reaching consequences in a certain country. The land mentioned was at the time of this writing deserted and barren, but it had once been "rich in fair pastures," and well populated with human kind. During a season, however, all this was changed by climatic disturbances which caused great numbers of spiders and scorpions to spring up. Whosoever was bitten by one of these creatures immediately died, and the populace rose up against them in terror. All efforts proved unavailing, however, and the people were forced to take flight to another country.

The Koran declares that "the likeness of those who choose other patrons than Allah is as the likeness of the spider when she taketh unto herself a house." The passage continues by emphasizing the weakness of the spider's abode. This intimates no antipathy to the creature itself, however, or to its habits when directed toward its own purposes. It merely uses it as a figure of speech, showing that those who depart from the Mohammedan faith are treading on an unstable foundation, insecure as a spider's web. The religious traditions of the Moslems revere the spider, and one of their sayings is that a spider once upon a time was instrumental in saving the life of Mohammed.

Spiders and their webs have been used for medicinal purposes from the time of Aristotle to the present era, and the early-day authors regarded the preparation as more than "charm medicine," or superstition. Dioscorides in the first century declared: "The house spider that spins a thick fine white web, shut up in a piece of leather or a nut-shell, and hanged to the arm or neck, is thought to drive away fits of quartan." Trallianus in the sixth century stated that "the fly-catching spider, wrapt in a linen cloth and hanged on the left arm, is good to drive away a quotidian. . . ." Spiders prepared in various ways and spider webs have been recommended as a cure for a fantastic assortment of ailments, including earache, tetters, running of the eyes, "wounds in the joints," warts, gout, ague, asthma, "spasmodic complaints of females," chronic hysteria, coughs, and "rheumatic affections of the head." Early writers, including Antonius Pius, and others subsequently, have utilized the web in stopping the flow of blood.

The spider has been chosen as a charm in numerous instances, and in others objects have been used to ward off "the evil effects from spiders." A belief was general in Germany during the sixteenth century, and held in many circles well into the seventeenth, according to Thorndyke, that the spider manufactured a stone which could be obtained only by dissecting the creature. Possession of a spider-stone was said to bring good fortune to its owner, and bestow upon him the gift of predicting future happenings. The "red agate," which is mentioned by Pliny and known as "blood agate," was employed as a protection against large spiders. A Norse legend tells that down in a shoal of a sea resided a monstrous spider called by some Kraken, and by others Fish-Mountain, which made a practice of seizing and sinking ships that came in its way.

Only certain rites (in which particular charms were used) performed by the seamen would prevent this ill fortune.

The literature is replete with many bizarre stories concerning spiders. Thorndyke relates that during the middle ages a scheme was formulated—but did not materialize—to poison a certain ecclesiastical personage of note by means of a solution containing spiders. He also recites a medieval account of a child who, at every opportunity, ran to secluded corners in the house and ate spiders. James tells of certain monks (living in a monastery in France) who died as a result of drinking out of a vessel in which a dead spider was subsequently discovered. He writes also of a woman who had a passion to destroy spiders. Once, as she was so doing, the spider "broke," and the creature's "fluids were thrown into her eyes and face." During the night the woman's lips swelled, one eye became much inflamed, and she vomited continually. It was several days before she recovered.

The British Isles have many traditions concerning spiders, some of which are based upon erroneous conceptions. The story of Robert Bruce and the Spider has become a classic in the English-speaking world. It is said that because of the good fortune it brought to him, "the people who live north of the Tweed will prevent you from killing a spider." There are many sayings based upon the erroneous assertion that the fauna of Ireland does not include spiders. That country is said to have contained no spiders since the island was cleared of all vermin by St. Patrick, and Savory quotes an anonymous poet: "Happy Ierne, whose most wholesome air poisons envenomed spiders. . . ." He also mentions a historical legend that in 1098 William II obtained by license of

Murchad, the Irish king, timber from the oak forest of Oxmantown, Dublin, which was used for the frames supporting the roof of Westminster Hall, "where no English spider webbeth or breedeth to this day." He likewise mentions the belief that spiders stay away from the King's College Chapel, Cambridge, which was built of Irish oak; and from oak this repugnance spread to cedar and chestnut, which latter was used, for that reason, to roof the parish church in Hambleton, Hampshire, in 1334.

Marco Polo, Shakespeare, Swift, Emerson, Southey, and Butler speak unfavorably of spiders in their writings. Marco Polo tells of a people who, upon seeing a certain spider—a *tarantula*—"take notice from which side it comes, and regulate their business accordingly." Shakespeare has the passage,

> *Weaving spiders, come not here,*
> *Hence, you long-legged spinners, hence!*

Swift dismisses the spider with a curt, "She produces nothing at all but flybane and a cobweb," while Emerson mentions spiders among the things to be expelled from the earth by the perfected man of the future. Southey uses the figure of speech,

> *Hell's huge black spider, for mankind he lays*
> *His toils, as those for flies.*

And Butler declares,

> *The subtle spider never spins,*
> *But on dark days, his slimy gins.*

W. H. Hudson narrates certain phases of the arachnid life of South America. He reveals that the natives fear some of the spiders, and that the feeling has been expressed in various forms. In particular, he mentions the gauchos' ballad "which tells that the city of Cordova was once invaded by an army of monstrous spiders, and that the townspeople went out with beating drums and flags flying to repel the invasion, but after firing several volleys they were forced to turn and fly for their lives."

In *Mother Goose*, and in other rhymes as well as lyrics of the kindergarten type, distrust of the spider is expressed. *The Spider and the Fly* and *Little Miss Muffet* are classics. What fears have taken hold in the plastic minds of children as a result of the recitation of these verses, only conjecture can answer. Some persons avow that these rhymes have caused no harm whatever, but that on the other hand the saying of them has afforded many pleasurable moments. Still others have asserted that such fantasies have been alarmingly injurious to the normal human attitude toward the tiny creatures of Arachnida and Insecta. However this may be, the spiders in these verses, to say the least, are not described as welcome visitors, but instead are pictured as crafty murderers luring insect victims into their lairs, or as creatures of terror sufficient to cause one to keep his distance.

Here in the United States folklore concerning spiders has been recorded by Curtis. The Indians who once populated the Great Lakes country (the Winnebagos) held a tradition concerning eight evil blind men who lived in a wood. They found their way around with the help of cords which they would wrap about the trees in the manner of a web, thereby capturing and slaughtering people. But one day Wash-ching-geka, The Little Hare, who was taken care of by his wise old grandmother, the Earth, placed poison in their bear meat, from which they died. Whereupon the eight wicked blind men were transformed into spiders, thus—so the narrative implies—expiating the horrible role which they had played.

According to Dane and Mary R. Coolidge, the Navajo Indians upon a time revered a mythical figure known as *The Spider Woman.* She it was who in the dawn of their history taught them how to make carrying baskets, water jars, and blankets. She specified that each blanket must be woven with a small hole in the center or, as the Indians (for commercial reasons) have explained it, in one of the diamonds, or concealed on the edge of the design. The Navajos have a phrase similar to our own "cobwebs in his brain." If the "tribute of the spider-hole" is denied the Spider Woman, they believe she will spin webs in the head of the weaver and destroy that worthy's mind.

Gifford and Block relate that the Luiseno Indians, once native of California, upon initiating their youth into the jimson-weed (Jameson) cult delivered lectures of paternal advice. They were narrated over a ground- or dry-painting, previously sketched on the ground with different colored sands and meals. The drawing consisted of the figures of various mythical celestial and terrestrial beings. The elders asserted that if a youth disobeyed their commands, one of the creatures pictured on the earth before them would do him harm. In one instance the counselors declared that the youth must neither steal food, nor eat hurriedly, nor overeat, and as a positive command, they instructed him to bathe immediately upon arising each morning. As a penalty for violating these rules, the wise men of the tribe admonished: "See here, this is a *black spider,* and it is going to bite you." On the other hand, should the youth heed them, then, according to the elders, "if a rattlesnake or *black spider* should bite you, you will not die."

The Spanish-speaking people of the Southwest, the authors have discovered, also possess a folklore concerning spiders, especially the Mexicans who inhabit that portion of the United States bordering old Mexico (as south and southwest Texas, the lower part of New Mexico and of Arizona, as well as southern California). Other stories pertain not alone to the spider itself, but equally well to the other small creatures of the desert fauna. Now and then there is a more direct reference to a particular spider, *la arana ponzonosa*; much fear is expressed concerning.

The southern Negro, according to Puckett, has fostered scores of myths and folk tales concerning spiders. These beliefs range from that which considers the spider as an omen to the saying that "the bite of any spider causes sickness and death." A spider dangling a certain way from its web may be thought of as a sign of good luck, the coming of a letter, the receipt of a sum of money, or the arrival of a visitor. A spider in yet another position may be considered as an omen of death in the family, loss of a cherished keepsake, or a quarrel with a neighbor. Many Negroes attribute almost any swelling or itching of unknown origin to the bite of a spider, and they have concocted divers cures for the same. The creature plays a unique role in the superstitions of the Negro of the South, but its significance falls short of the belief held by certain natives of Africa who regard the spider as the creator of all men, at the same time contending that it is supposed to speak through the nose as the local demons are alleged to do.

Enquiries by the authors show that spider folklore likewise prevails among multitudes of the white people of the South and Southwest, and also of the North and Northwest. Some of it concerns spiders and their spinning work, and there are fireside tales extolling their skill in this wise. Other stories revolve around the fact that, in some instances, letters of the alphabet can be read in the spider's web. A belief still set forth in a certain county in Kentucky, as related by D. L. and L. B. Thomas, is that President McKinley's death was prophesied in spiders' webs. Many persons of North Carolina during the summer of 1914, and again in 1917, were said to have seen series of "W's" in the webs of garden spiders. They averred that these letters began words which foretold numerous events of world-wide importance. A widely disseminated and popular belief is that spiders prognosticate weather changes. This notion was entertained as early as the days of Pliny, and variations of the ancient conception are found in the South. Other tales relate to the appearance of spiders, and still others to their poison qualities.

The foregoing indicates that mankind has both favored and loathed spiders. There are several reasons for the former attitude. History shows that humankind has, from time to time, connected most creatures of field and forest with superstitious beliefs. Thus the spider has been thought of as a charm, an omen of good luck, and a weather forecaster. Spiders possess a utilitarian value in that their webs are used for criss-cross hairs in telescopic gun and bomb sights, range-finders, and optical instruments. Attempts have been made by Wilder and others to utilize the spider's silk in the weaving of fabrics, but the ventures proved impracticable for commercial purposes.

We have seen that spiders and their webs have been used for medicinal purposes. Many people enjoy watching spiders spin their webs, and naturalists have long contended that their habits hold an enticing interest. Spiders destroy insects that are injurious to plants and man, and therefore help in maintaining the balance of nature.

There are also reasons why hosts of people dislike spiders. The unusual number of legs, the hairy appearance of large spiders, and the peculiar eyes may play a role. Many of the species may be observed as they snare their prey, and the sight of this may cause some individuals to abhor spiders. House spiders spin their webs in any convenient corner and are therefore considered a pest by the tidy housewife. Abandoned houses, as well as dwelling places occupied by the eccentric, often have strands of spider web streaming from the ceiling, clouding a section of the windowpane, or bridging empty flower pots on a veranda shelf.

A further reason why people look with disfavor upon spiders is that there exist throughout the world species which belong to the same genus as the dangerous black widow—*Latrodectus*. It may logically be conceived that in many communities individuals have been bitten by members of *Latrodectus* and thereby endured much suffering. It is not hard to believe that the layman, aware of such cases, but not being able to distinguish one genus from the other, has concluded that nearly all spiders are capable of inflicting painful bites upon human beings. Hence it is desirable to determine which spiders are dangerous to man, and to point out the significance of the genus *Latrodectus* in the history of spider bites.

2. Tarantism

wwwwwwwwwwwwwwwwwwwwwwwwwwwwwwwwwwwwwwwwwwwwwwwwwwwwwwwwwwwwwwwwwwwwwwwwwwwwwwwwwwwwwww

IN ITALY—particularly in the southern portion about the vicinity of Taranto—there existed a spider scare which reached its height in the seventeenth century, but which endured much later and still persists among certain sections of the peasants. Many persons were said to have been affected with a disease (*tarantism, tarentism, tarantulism*) resulting from having been bitten (*tarantulated*) by a species of wolf spider, *Lycosa tarantula*. To rid the body of the venom, the patients (*tarantists, tarantatii*) engaged in a lively dance which became known as the *tarantella*.

We shall discuss first, the dance "cure," and then, the spider. Fiction, lore, and factual history all tell of the former, and they reveal that the mania in Italy was preceded by a craze which arose in the fourteenth century as an aftermath of the Black Death and swept Germany, Belgium, Switzerland, France, and England. The *Scientific American* refers to an old account which states that men and women formed circles and danced hour after hour in wild delirium, some of the performers afterwards vowing that they felt as if they had been immersed in a stream of blood. Westen narrates the story that two hundred fanatics began to dance on the Mosel Bridge at

Utrecht and would not stop until a priest passed by carrying the Host. The bridge subsequently gave way, and all were drowned. He further relates that eighteen peasants disturbed divine service on Christmas day near the convent church of Kolbig, and the priest, pronouncing a curse, told them that they should dance and scream without ceasing for a period of twelve months. They at length sank knee deep into the earth but were released by the intercession of two bishops, only to fall into a profound sleep from which there was no awakening. Hecker states that in certain instances the dancing epidemic produced a longing on the part of some participants for the sea, and they cast themselves into it and were drowned; that other afflicted ones lapsed into profound melancholy, wandering into churchyards and finding solace in the tolling of the funeral bell; and not a few gained relief by burying themselves up to their necks in the earth among the tombstones. The tales range from descriptions of the performers dashing their brains out against the walls and corners of buildings or throwing themselves into rivers or convenient wells to drown, to the ordinance passed at the insistence of dancing devotees that no shoemaker was to make any but "square-toed shoes."

In Italy music played an important role in the dancing. So widespread was the enthusiasm for music therapy during the seventeenth century that a pretentious work appeared, entitled *Magis Universalis Naturae et Artis*, which contained measures of music that supposedly acted as an antidote for the bite of *Lycosa tarantula*. Various municipalities hired special musicians to play for the dancers as well as a corps of substitutes to relieve the regular accompanists as they became exhausted. Their services were

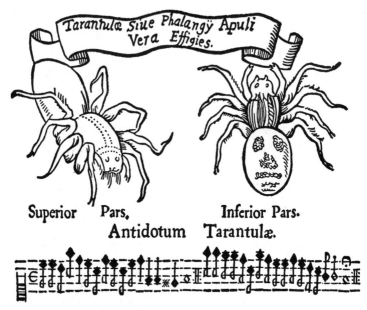

Superior Pars.
Antidotum Tarantulæ.
Inferior Pars.

In southern Italy there existed a spider scare which reached its height in the seventeenth century. Persons supposedly bitten by a species of wolf spider, Lycosa tarantula, were said to be cured only after indulging in a lively dance which became known as the tarantella. This is a copy of an early-day music sheet showing the first few bars of the dance.—Bettman Archive.

frequently demanded during the summer months, particularly in the dog-days, as the spiders at that season were said to be most abundant. Pepys mentioned the musical cure and testified that one Mr. Templer, "a great traveler," informed him that "all the harvest long there are fiddlers who go up and down the fields everywhere, in expectations of being hired by those who are stung."

Concerning southern Europe, the accounts of the dancing are legion, and varied in details. Savory cites the narrative which speaks of a woman dancer springing up with a "hideous yell" once the chord supposed to vibrate her heart had been touched. "She staggered about the room like a drunken person, holding a handkerchief in both hands, raising them alternately, and moving in very true time." *Once a Week* summarizes an early account which tells that alleged victims of spider bite "are as men half dead, but at first sound of a musical instrument they begin by degrees to move their hands and feet, till at last they get up, and then fall to dancing with wonderful vigor for two or three hours, their strength and activity continually increasing." McCook cites a description which states that a purported spider-bit victim "leaped and danced incessantly to the accompaniment of music, but once it stopped he fell to the ground as if dead." When, however, the musicians began to play again "he mounted upon his feet, and danced as lustily as formerly, till he found himself entirely recovered."

It came about that those who made no pretense of being bitten sometimes manifested the accepted symptoms of tarantism, and inquisitive persons who came to see the dance participated. The many accounts describe the dance in all its phases, including the attire of the performers, the decorations of the space set aside for the exhibitions, the individual behavior of the actors, and the reactions of the spectators.

That the dances occurred there is no doubt. The craze is a part of history. But the cause of their occurrence is another matter, and in deciding that, it is best to inquire into the purported influence of *Lycosa tarantula* and its bite. It is actually a common species of spider, and certainly there is no mystery connected with it at the present time. Its genus name, *Lycosa*, is Greek for *wolf*, and the *Lycosidae* leap upon their insect-prey in the manner of their namesake. Its species title, *tarantula*, is derived from Taranto, the Italian city in the vicinity of which the creatures are supposed to be prolific. The application of the term *tarantula* to any large spider, as the hairy creatures of the southwestern and western United States, is a misnomer, but usage has decreed that this remain their popular name. Rightly speaking, and from a priority standpoint, *tarantula* should be used in connection only with the *Lycosa* spiders of that species.

The next question concerns the potency of the bite of *Lycosa tarantula*. Diogenes (404–323 B.C.) spoke of its being able to bring death to mankind, and through subsequent centuries both great and small minds have thus attested. Nicholas Perotti in an account of tarantism pointed out that "no one had the least doubt that it was caused by the bite of this spider." Drs. Mead in England, Burette in France, and Baghlivi in Italy regarded *L. tarantula's* bite as dangerous to man, and prescribed the dancing treatment as a cure. The last-named wrote a special treatise, in which we find set down the airs most suited to effect a cure. *Once a Week* states that an early writer asserted that the poison of this spider when injected into a human being "thickens the blood and stops several of its passages. . . ."

In time, however, skeptics began to doubt that *L. tarantula's* bite was as dangerous as stated. Cornelio represented tarantism as an imaginary disease; Abbe Nollet affirmed that it was not due to spider bite; and Dumerit declared it to be an unreality. Oliver Goldsmith, while visiting Italy, attended the dances and, as a bit of scientific detection, caused a servant to be bitten by *Lycosa tarantula*.

There was no injurious result. Fabre testified that its poison is not serious to man, "and causes less inconvenience than a gnat-bite." Lankester, Wood, Comstock, Savory, McCook, Simon, and other naturalists have minimized the effects of the bite of *L. tarantula*, either by stating that they were practically nil or of such insignificance as to cause no alarm. Vellard reports that the bite of a South American species, *L. raptoria*, may cause marked symptoms in a human being. The authors have experimented with a large species of *Lycosa* which inhabits certain adobe hills within the vicinity of Los Angeles, and found that the creature bites vigorously without coaxing. The wound punctures when penetrating a tender portion of the skin are annoying but not painful. Medical men have made controlled testings, and they discredit the belief that *L. tarantula* caused suffering to masses of humanity in Europe. It is now known that the bite of *Lycosa* may produce severe local lesions, but with little systemic accompaniment.

Because of this, therefore, it is necessary to review the theories that have been offered to explain the "dancing madness." Some contemporaries considered the malady as "the work of a devil, and the clergy were kept busy in their efforts to exorcise the evil one." Certain later investigators explain that the mania originated in the ancient peasant custom of dancing in churchyards—which were also graveyards. A third group of theorists assert that the dancing mania swept the whole of Europe as a result of "mob psychology"; a fourth declares that the dance was utilized as an outlet for pent-up emotions; a fifth bears upon the fact that attendants about the dancing arena made a practice of asking for contributions, hence the affair was merely a bait for tourists; a sixth states that the climate of Taranto tends "to cause nervous affections," and that the dance came into being as a tonic to offset this; and still another avows that the dancers were adherents of the ancient cult of Bacchus, hence they used the excuse of spider bite to cover up the actual reason for their behavior.

Some of these hypotheses may account for a portion of the recorded instances of dancing, but there are many cases which they do not adequately explain. One account declares that an adult male patient "was sorely afflicted with violent symptoms, as syncopes, very great agitation, giddiness of the head, and vomiting, but that without a desire of having any musical instrument." Another narrative speaks of the patients as being affected with "violent sickness, difficulty of breathing, fainting, and sometimes trembling." These cases involved persons who were actually ill. The symptom picture strikingly resembles that of patients who have been bitten by *Latrodectus*. A spider actually may have been involved. *Latrodectus tridecimguttatus*, or *malmignatte*, thrives in the vicinity of Taranto. It is possible that they mingled with the other spiders of field and forest and at times struck their fangs into the harvesters. The latter, seeking a culprit, discovered only the larger and more abundant *Lycosidae*, while *Latrodectus*, having struck unseen, scuttled to safety. Vellard concurs in this conclusion. However the case may be, *Latrodectus malmignatte* is the only species of spider in southern Italy the bite of which is capable of causing severe, systemic symptoms in a human being.

ABOVE: A species of Lycosa (wolf spider). They derive their name from the fact that they leap upon their insect-prey in the manner of a wolf. One similar to the above, Lycosa tarantula, thrives in Italy within the vicinity of Taranto. The cure for its alleged bite was the tarantelle dance, which developed into a craze that reached its height the middle of the 17th century. It is now known, however, that Lycosa tarantula's poison is harmless to man. Exact size.—Photos by Newton Berlin.

BELOW: A close-up of the so-called tarantula (Eurypelma californica). This spider is feared by many people, but its poison lacks potency sufficient under normal circumstances to produce permanent or serious harm to man. One-half natural size.

ABOVE: *Closed trapdoor to a trapdoor spider's nest, which is made to appear like its surroundings by being camouflaged with dirt, sticks, and grass. One-half natural size.—Photos by Newton Berlin.*

The opened trapdoor to a trapdoor spider's abode. It is bevel-edged, and when closed fits snugly into the neck of the abode. The tunnel extends down to a depth of ten to twelve inches, and, like the under side of the door, is lined with web. One-half natural size.

Trapdoor spider of Southern California (Bothriocyrtum californicum). Trapdoor spiders are to be found in Central and South America, portions of continental Europe, and other parts of the world. Under normal conditions, symptoms in man resulting from their bite will be local, and these spiders as a class cannot be considered greatly dangerous. Exact size.—Photos by Newton Berlin.

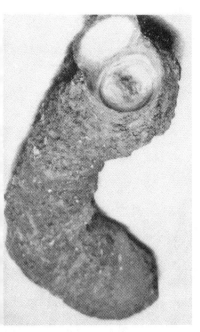

Excavated burrow of California trapdoor spider. About ten inches long.

Showing upper portion of trapdoor spider's burrow, which was dug out of the earth. The hole at the edge of the door may have been drilled by a natural enemy of this spider, as a wasp. This tube was found empty, except for a few spider carcass parts. About one-fourth natural size.

ABOVE: Two tarantulas having come upon an insect prey at the identical moment, they tear into one another. One-half natural size. —Photos by Newton Berlin.

BELOW: A quintet of tarantula spiders native to California sparring with each other. These creatures battle each other to death upon the slightest provocation, but won't bite man unless teased at length. One-fifth natural size.

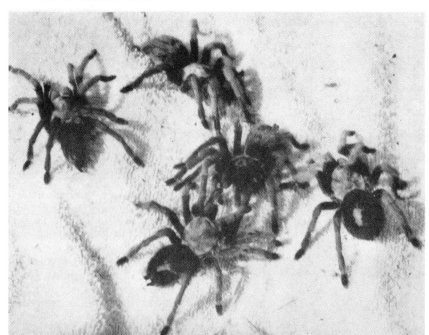

3. Other Poisonous Spiders

〜〜〜〜〜〜〜〜〜〜〜〜〜〜〜〜〜〜〜〜〜〜〜〜〜〜〜〜〜〜〜〜〜〜〜〜

THERE are a number of other species of spiders throughout the world which have been reported as causing suffering to man. The oft-mentioned "banana" spider has been an especial target for critics who are ignorant of spiders in general. One of the most frequently committed errors is made by those who refer to this creature as a "tarantula," as in reality it is not one, nor even related. It is instead one of the giant crab spiders and belongs to the family *Heteropodidae*. On the other hand, it is comparable in size to a few of the smaller specimens of tarantulas, and its eight long legs, which extend laterally from the body, make this spider appear gargantuan. The "banana" spider is a tropical species which frequently arrives in the United States hidden in bunches of bananas.

There are recorded cases in which man has been bitten by one of this species, but in each instance the maximum effects hardly compare with a serious case of black widow spider bite. In a communication to the authors, P. W. Fattig of Emory University, Atlanta, Georgia, tells of his having been bitten accidentally by a banana spider, *Heteropoda venatoria*. "My finger was swollen to twice its natural size within two minutes," he writes. "Sharp pains were felt to my shoulder. This pain and swelling lasted

for about two hours. No ill effects." In a separate investigation concerning the banana spider, but reaching a
conclusion to which the above might well be a contributing example, Ewing summarizes, "Its bite is sharply painful, but not dangerous."

In Australia the bite of *Atrax formidabilis* and *Atrax
robustus* may cause severe symptoms in a human being,
and under certain conditions, death. Especially is this
true of the latter species, which, however, is limited in
its distribution. Ingram and Musgrave, writing of its being
found in New South Wales, report fatal cases, and Beasley
lists a death. McKeown describes it as the "spider with the
darkest reputation in Australia." He points out that it is
not a trap-door spider, as asserted by popular writers, but
a funnel-web spider. Excluding the legs, the female measures up to one and one-half inches in length, and the
male, one inch. "Both sexes are ebony black, with the
forepart of the body highly polished and glossy, while
the soft abdomen is densely covered with a velvety pile.
The under surface of the body bears tufts and brushes of
grizzled red hair." He relates that in February, 1927, a
two-year-old boy was bitten by one of these spiders and
died within one hour and a half. "Three other deaths
occurred between that date and January, 1933; these were
a little girl of five years, who died in one and a quarter
hours, and two women, aged forty-seven and twenty-six,
who died in eleven and thirteen hours respectively. Three
cases of recovery are also on record for the same period,
and in each the patient was at first desperately ill. . . ."

In South America a number of species have been singled
out as enemies of mankind in varying degrees. Vellard
made extensive investigations concerning the giant *My-*

gales, as well as aquatic, house, and other families of spiders. Several dangerous species are mentioned by name, and they include *Polybetes maculatus, Selenops spixii,* and *Acanthoscurria sternalis.* Vellard tested their venom on various creatures, including pigeons, guinea pigs, rabbits, mice, white rats, batrachia (Paludicola), snakes (young *Lachesis jararaca*), lizards (*Lygosoma*), and a toad (*Bufo marinus*). In some instances the animal died within five, ten, or fifteen minutes following the injection of the spider poison; in others, after as much as thirty-six hours had elapsed; and in still other instances, recovery took place. These variations depended partly upon the species of test subject, as well as the spider used to supply the venom. Vellard also recorded case histories of man, and, while fatalities are rare, severe local lesion, edema, paralysis, necrosis, anaesthesia of the bitten member and other symptoms may follow the bite of certain species of spiders. The largest of the world's spiders is the South American *Theraphosa leblondi,* some with a body measuring as much as three and one-half inches in length. It is related to the so-called tarantula of the United States.

Baerg likewise has experimented with those huge spiders which around the globe are commonly called tarantulas. They occur throughout Mexico, Central America, Puerto Rico, Haiti, San Domingo, Martinique, Java, Africa, Madagascar, and elsewhere. Baerg states that he has made various tests with at least fourteen species which inhabit Central and North America, and all but two of these may be described as essentially harmless to man. "A large dark brown or blackish species (*Sericopelma communis*) occurring in Panama may be considered poisonous, though perhaps not dangerously so. On man the bite, with about a half a dose of poison, produces moderate swelling and rather severe pain. The effects are, however, local and readily subside if the bitten hand is immersed in hot water. . . . Another poisonous, or at least a doubtful case, is a species of tarantula occurring near Santiago, state of Nayarit, Mexico. It is characterized by a warm brown color of the tibiae (probably *Eurypelma emilia*). Two tests have been made with white rats and both ended fatally. . . ."

Within the United States there are trap-door spiders—both those building a wafer-type and those building a cork-type lid for their web-coated burrows—which have been thought of by the layman as dangerous to man. Sixteen species have been found and of these, eight are recorded exclusively from California. Others are found throughout the southern and southwestern states, with one species being discovered as far north in Virginia as the Potomac. Trap-door spiders are to be found in Central and South America, portions of continental Europe, and other parts of the world. Their ill reputation, however, does not compare with that of the species of the genus *Latrodectus*, although death is reported to have occurred following the bite of a Texas trap-door spider. Under normal conditions, symptoms resulting from the bite of the trap-door spider will be local, and these spiders as a class cannot be considered as greatly dangerous to man.

The most feared spider in the United States other than the black widow is the so-called tarantula, a monstrous, hairy creature that belongs to the *Aviculariidae* family. It is found throughout the South and Southwest, and has a life span of as much as twenty-five years. Rumors concerning its "deadly" bite are constantly arising, hence we shall examine in detail both lay and scientific testimony.

The literature concerning them is comprehensive. These giant spiders have been mentioned by various writers since Hentz's time (the first half of the nineteenth century). William Lewis Manly of Death Valley fame, Charles C. Abbott, the New England essayist, Major Horace Bell, a chronicler of California history, William H. Brewer, noted scientist from the Sheffield Scientific School at Yale, Kate Sanborn, a narrator of fact and whimsical humor, and many other early-day writers wrote of the tarantula. In almost every instance they mentioned the general fear of the creature, but their statements failed to detail case histories of patients who had fallen victims to the creature's bite. Literature concerning the tarantula published before the turn of the century dealt in part with tradition and superstition, partly with alleged observations which were patently false, and the remainder with hearsay reports.

Some of the early-day accounts may be placed in the class exemplified by an incident which occurred near San Pedro, California, twenty-four miles from the heart of Los Angeles. On a certain Fourth of July many years ago when the country between the two cities was little other than pasture land, a band of mustangs quartered there broke loose and stampeded. Neighboring ranchers attributed the stampede to an imaginary creature which they termed the phantom tarantula. The more scientific-minded individuals, however, were not satisfied with this explanation. Investigating, they learned that a certain citizen had imbibed too greatly while in San Pedro, and, on his way back to Los Angeles, toppled from his sulky onto the trail-side. His trusty nag noted its master's condition and wandered off the road into better grazing grounds, paying little attention to the grotesque vehicle which dangled ever to the rear. The band of mustangs, some distance from their owners, espied the cumbersome contraption, and with neighs of alarm galloped pell-mell in diverse directions. Thus the phantom tarantula was explained away, and in this case where superstition played the dominant role there was little association with the creature itself other than the appropriation of its name.

Many frontier-day folk tales concerning the tarantula are based upon an early "remedy" for the bite of the creature. In a certain region of the Southwest, it was long held that whiskey was the one successful treatment for tarantula bite, and in connection therewith the worst sort of liquor, formerly known as "Taos lightning," had its name perverted into "tarantula juice." It was said of one old Indian that he loved the cure so much that he carried around a "tame" tarantula, and frequently found it convenient to get bitten near a grocery store. At such times he would exhibit the spider as a proof that he had been bitten, and "howled around," so a contemporary stated, "until he was gratuitously irrigated with the worthy antidote." In this, little analysis is needed to see that the subject of these incidents was the instigator of a hoax, and from the known evidence there is no proof that he was ever bitten by a tarantula.

Another of the early-day writings may be placed in a category such as was illustrated by a contemporary woman correspondent. She stated that during 1929, while she was employed in a certain cafe in the town of Gila Bend, Arizona, "a report came in that caused everyone to shudder." She explained further that a man with a "very high forehead" was working under his car when something dropped down onto his forehead. "This he at first supposed to be a leaf or a portion of weed, but in brushing it off, he learned that it was a tarantula. The big spider did not bite him," the woman opined, "but everywhere its feet had touched his forehead there were livid spots." Subsequently his "face swelled until his features were scarcely distinguishable," and, she asserted, "a week later he was still a dreadful looking sight with his nose just showing that it was really there." This is a fair sample of ridiculous tales of the tarantula, whose walking appendages are not equipped with anything resembling a poison device, and therefore could not have produced such symptoms.

Still other of the nineteenth-century comments may be classified as similar to a published interview with a person in a southwestern state who was considered most adept at catching tarantulas. On his expeditions he had a corps of assistants, one of whom would proceed ahead of the rest and place a small red flag at the opening of the spider's nest. Another assistant would pour a quantity of water into the burrow of the creature, upon which it would rush to the surface of the earth to investigate. At this point in the procedure the expert tarantula huntsman, standing in readiness close at hand, would seize the spider with a pair of pincers and thrust it into a bottle. This nature student told his interviewer "that there seems to be a general impression that a tarantula will jump into a second-story window of a house, and, springing upon the neck of a young lady sitting there, will kill her instantly." While this account may contain a note of satire, it nevertheless indicates the modern trend of public opinion regarding the tarantula, and that viewpoint is, in most instances, expressed by persons who have made no practical research regarding the bite of the tarantula.

Finally, other of the pioneer references may be classified as analogous to the statements made by a certain investigator who, although a member of a geological expedition to California in 1860–64, studied what he termed the "dreadful tarantula." In writing to his friends in the East, he noted: "I have seen them so large that two would cover this page, as they stand. Their bodies are as large as a half-grown mouse; their hairy legs of proportionate size; their fangs as large as those of a moderate sized rattlesnake. Pleasant companions! We never think of pulling on our boots in the morning without first shaking them, for fear of tarantulas. . . . They bite vigorously when provoked, and their bite is generally considered fatal. . . ." Despite the seriousness of the charge against the tarantula as contained in this last statement, and despite the fact that the assertion warrants further consideration, it is in the nature of a mere declaration, and no tangible proof has been offered as to its reliability.

In the literature, however, there are definite listings of tarantula bite cases. In the year 1901 Browning sent out a questionnaire to a number of physicians in southern California concerning venomous creatures, particularly those belonging to the class Arachnida. Information was thus obtained covering the bites of five tarantulas as well as reports on seventy black widow spider-bite cases. This ratio of tarantula to black widow bites (one to fourteen) would be far less if today a survey were taken in the same locality. Encroaching civilization, represented by increased building of human habitations on land where "tarantula towns" existed, has resulted in the rooting out of the gigantic subterranean spiders. The tarantula has thus been deprived of suitable areas in which to burrow her den, and the houses and auxiliary buildings have provided numerous protective abodes for the black widow spider. Nationally, the tarantula (in comparison to the black widow) is numerically insignificant, since the former is confined to certain portions of a few Western states, while the latter's scope is boundless.

The second phase in determining the poison potentialities of the tarantula is concerned with instances where man has played guinea pig to this spider. We find that in addition to our own personal observations, there are no less than three cases where individuals have tested the tarantula's venom upon their own persons. In 1922 Baerg induced a large female tarantula, *Eurypelma steindachneri*, to strike him twice on the inside of the small finger of the left hand. In the first attempt the fangs barely penetrated the skin, but when the test was repeated, one fang went well under the skin, just below the first joint. The sensation produced by the strike was like that following the stab of a pin, and within less than an hour all traces of pain disappeared. "At no time was the finger at all stiff," comments Baerg. The following day the test was again attempted. The same tarantula was used. With but little hesitation she struck twice, and in about the same place as before. This time, however, the supply of venom was more generous, two large drops collecting and running down the sides of the finger. The pain was similar to that in the first test, and within two hours all traces of it had disappeared. Although Baerg, as pointed out by himself, did not get what could be considered a good dose, the symptoms nevertheless led him to conclude that normally "the bite of a tarantula is not dangerous to man. . . ."

In 1928 Ewing recorded some observations concerning a tarantula, *Eurypelma californica* Ausserer, which he had possessed since 1924. It had been lodged in a wire cage. During the years it was handled by many people, and struck only once. That occurred when a woman observer caught the creature rather carelessly as it crawled over her shoulder, and, as Ewing believes, accidentally squeezed it. The tarantula sank its fangs into the tip of the second finger. A drop of blood collected at the punctured point and dropped onto the floor. Blood continued to flow during an interval of several minutes. Although the patient spoke of considerable pain, which she likened to that produced by the stab of a pin, there was no swelling, and after an hour all symptoms disappeared. Ewing believes the results of the bite represented only mechanical injury.

But he was not satisfied and later experimented upon himself. After chloroforming a large tarantula, he removed a fang, and, with the poison sac laid bare, forced it into the left arm. At the moment no poison was ejected. To overcome this deficiency, the fang was held between the finger and the thumb under the binocular microscope, and a drop of poison was squeezed out by means of pressure on the sac. This drop was placed on the puncture previously made by the fang, and the latter was thrust into the flesh until the blood came. There was, in addition to very mild symptoms, some smarting and soreness of the arm, but after four hours Ewing was able to report that all noticeable effects had disappeared. He states his belief that if a large amount of the venom were injected into a small child there likely would be much pain and discomfort, but in referring to adults he asserts that "the bite of this tarantula would probably not be serious."

P. W. Fattig reports his personal experiment with the tarantula's bite. It required thirty minutes of teasing and coaxing on his part to induce a very large specimen to sink its fangs into his thumb. They entered to a depth of about one quarter inch, and he permitted them to remain there for about three minutes in order to receive the maximum quantity of poison from the spider. He reported the following results: "Although my finger felt as if it were swollen to about twice its natural size, which feeling lasted for about three hours, I could hardly detect any visible sign of swelling." The pain approximated that of two or three simultaneous honey bee stings, and endured for approximately two hours. "There was no illness caused from the bite," summarized Fattig. "There was no change in respiration or heart beat. In fact, I could not determine any effect at all, except the slight pain, and the sensation of swelling."

Beginning in 1933, and in subsequent years, we together with our helpers have handled many hundreds of tarantulas, the majority of them belonging to the species *Eurypelma californica* and the remainder to species *E. steindachneri*, *E. marxi*, *E. hentzi* and *E. rusticum*. One of our aides, a youth gifted in nature study, and now twenty years of age, has collected many hundreds of tarantulas for us. His method is to carry a jug of water to the chosen locality, and upon locating a burrow (which in circumference is about the size of a silver dollar and has a pyramid of freshly dug earth about the entrance), to pour a quantity of the water into the hole. In most instances no more than a pint of the liquid is necessary to cause the creature to come rushing head foremost to the entrance. When near the rim the tarantula usually halts, which act undoubtedly is one of precaution in determining what has caused the deluge. At this point in the proceedings it is our practice to insert a stick under the creature, with a quick movement flipping it out of the burrow and onto the surface of the earth. Our youthful assistant does not, however, depend upon the stick to get the creature out and into the open. He instead reaches down into the burrow and takes hold of it with his finger tips, pulls it out and inserts it into a cigar box or other receptacle which has been brought along for the purpose. Upon no less than three occasions, in all of which we were eye witnesses, this young man was bitten by the tarantula in hand. In each instance we observed the creature as it struck, and afterward examined the fang holes, notwithstanding which he shrugged off each accident with the words: "The pain is nothing; it's just like being stuck with a pin."

In connection with the above, we have discovered that certain species of tarantulas found in the United States bite only after continued provocation. We have often allowed specimens to crawl upon our hands and arms. Upon one occasion when one of us was preparing a magazine assignment which demonstrated the comparative harmlessness of this spider, he permitted photographs to be made showing a tarantula clinging to his left cheek. At another time, for the edification of friends, we repeatedly teased and irritated a specimen with the rubber end of a pencil. This was continued for fully twenty-five minutes, during which time the spider did not bare its fangs. Finally, in a spirit of humaneness toward such creatures of the wild, and at the pleas of our audience—who, moreover, were overwhelmingly convinced of this tarantula's apathy—we ceased our annoyance of the spider.

We therefore see that tarantulas of the United States cannot be accepted as a menace. They are slow to attack a human being, are not numerous, and their poison lacks potency sufficient under normal circumstances to produce permanent or even serious harm. Mankind has reacted in some instances to poison secreted by certain species, as the giant *Mygales* of South America, but simple, local treatment is usually all that is necessary to offset the temporary effects. The bite of *Atrax robustus* of Australia, however, may cause serious symptoms and, under certain conditions, death to man. Fortunately this species is limited in its range; hence few instances of this kind are on record. The most universally distributed "dangerous" spiders are those of the genus *Latrodectus*, and it is they, more than all others, which are responsible for serious cases of spider bite.

4. *Latrodectus Around the World*

~~~~~~

THE GENUS *Latrodectus* is found in each of the five continents. Several species are represented in North America. In the United States *L. geometricus* has been discovered in Florida and California, but the most frequently mentioned is *L. mactans*, popularly known as the black widow spider. She has received much newspaper publicity, her presence has been reported in each of the forty-eight states, and efforts by man have been made to control her propagation. Scores of case histories have been reported by physicians, the symptom picture has been established, and treatments have been formulated. It has been determined that the bite of *L. mactans* may cause severe, systemic pain in a human being, and under certain conditions death may result.

Indians in several instances definitely referred to *L. mactans*. It is now an accepted fact, according to Chamberlin and Ivie, that some of the Utah Indians (the Gosiutes) occasionally mixed the macerated bodies of the black widow spiders with liver already impregnated with the poison of the rattlesnake. With this concoction they smeared their arrow heads. There is also a specific mention of the spider in the Indian myths collected by Dr. C. Hart Merriam. He states that the California Indians (the

Northern Mewuk) knew *L. mactans* as Po-ko-moo. They, in referring to the "small black spider with a red spot under his belly," asserted that it "scratches people with his long fingers, and the scratch makes a bad sore." Dr. Merriam relates further that upon questioning the Indians of California, he learned that it has been their custom to make use of the black widow's poison by mashing up entire spiders and, after mixing them with several other ingredients, dipping the points of their arrowheads into the resulting concoction. It is unlikely, however, that such material did more than increase the chances of infection from wounds.

The presence of *Latrodectus* has been reported within the Canadian provinces of Alberta, British Columbia, Manitoba, and Ontario. In the West Indies there is the spider known colloquially as *cul rouge*; actually, science recognized two species as inhabiting those islands—*L. curacaviensis* and *L. geometricus*. Central America harbors the species mentioned in the literature as *cassampulga* or *pallu*, and within the latter two areas there have long existed numerous legends concerning *Latrodectus*, some of which contain details indicating that they are based upon fact. But more than this, *Latrodectus* in these portions of the globe has been studied from both arachnological and clinical viewpoints, and her career, regardless of the species, has much in common with *L. mactans* of the United States.

In Mexico, *Latrodectus* is familiar to portions of the native population, and they look upon her with awe. In that country a species of *Latrodectus* is designated by the Mexicans as *arana capulina*, "the cherry spider," and by certain of the Indians as *chintatlahue*. Some tribal doctors of the interior assert that the spider is dangerous, but not necessarily deadly, declaring that her bite may incite a fatigue in the human body that will endure for several days. On the other hand, some natives state that the bite will cause certain death unless the tribal cure is immediately administered. This cure is described as a bean of allegedly the same shape and size as the body of the spider; and in color half white and half black. The bean is powdered, mixed with water, and administered as a gruel.

Within recent times, a mere rumor of the presence of *Latrodectus* played an unusual role in Mexico. With the black widow spider receiving attention from the newspapers of the United States, the journalists of Mexico decided that what was meat and drink for others was also grist for their mill. The most alarming account appeared in a Torreon paper, which in its initial item proclaimed that black widow spiders were invading the community. On the following day the heading ran, *Siembran el Panico* (The Panic Continues).

While in this instance imagination rather than fact proved to be the foundation for the articles, nevertheless there have been case histories recorded in Mexico. Some of these, to be sure, were not reported by competent observers, but there have been reliable reports. In 1921 Turpin of Esmeralda, Coahuila, mentioned having been bitten by a small, black spider with a white cross on her back. The symptoms in a number of respects resembled those from the bite of *L. mactans*, and Turpin testified that he "seldom had more severe pain." In 1921, Louis of San Juan, Coahuila, wrote of a black spider with a few "white spots" on her body. And he mentioned four cases resulting from the bite of the creature, in each of which the most noticeable symptom was pain.

In South America, *Latrodectus* has been observed by both layman and scientist in Brazil, Argentina, Chile, Bolivia, Uruguay, and Peru, actually from the northern part of that continent southward to Tierra del Fuego. From conversations with persons familiar with the South American fauna, we have learned of the fear with which the native population regards this spider and the superstition with which it has enveloped her. Some of the natives of Chile believe that the spider bites only on specified days, and that only evil persons will suffer or die as a result of the injected poison. In other sections of the same country the belief is held that the spider will remain aloof from one's house provided a certain root is burned in an open container, and particular words are mumbled. It is imperative that this ceremony be conducted by the tribal doctor. Many of the inhabitants of Argentina aver that the spider preys upon children, especially those whose parents have not been obedient to certain religious precepts. A lore has been developed by some of the Indians in Peru that *Latrodectus* comes at stated periods as an inevitable plague and that little can be done to stave off such depredations.

A knowledge of these beliefs, coupled with an insatiable scientific curiosity, has prompted not a few learned men of South America to investigate the spider-bite question, and to record their findings. More than forty writers, including Houssay, Mazza, Brazil, Troise, and Escomel, have published reports concerning arachnidism. Observations of *Latrodectus* have been made in the field, with the result that the color design and external anatomy of the spider, the locations of her nest and its pattern, and her foraging and nuptial tactics have been noted. The effects of the bite of the spider on man have been studied in clinic and laboratory, with the result that numerous case histories have been chronicled, the symptom picture has been established, and serums and other forms of treatment have been promulgated. The conclusion has been reached that the bite of *Latrodectus* of South America may cause intense suffering to man, and under certain conditions death may result.

Of particular significance have been the studies of Vellard. Both his knowledge of medicine and his qualifications as a naturalist enabled him to investigate *Latrodectus* thoroughly. Vellard states that *L. mactans*, the black widow spider of the United States, prevails in Chile, Argentina, Uruguay, and to a lesser degree in Peru, Venezuela, and other countries of the tropics.

There thrives another species in South America, *L. geometricus*, which is widely distributed, but her record of causing suffering to man is less than that attributed to *L. mactans*. Vellard describes *L. geometricus* as 10 to 12 mm. in length and ranging in color from light to dark gray, with the presence of a variable amount of buff or brown in her general coloration. She constructs a tuberculated egg case, and her web consists of coarse, criss-cross strands. She weaves her nest at the base of plants and between the low branches as well as in other out-of-door places, and also in any convenient niche about human habitations.

Vellard classified the venom of *Latrodectus* as neurotoxic. He tested it upon various animals and noted that death of the victim often, but not always, resulted from the injected poison. He stated that in regions where these spiders are abundant they frequently bite man, and death sometimes follows. The symptoms include severe, systemic pain, muscle spasm, and profuse perspiration, together with nervousness and anxiety to the point that several patients felt as if they were going insane.

In Europe there is a record that tells of suffering and death from the bite of several species of *Latrodectus*. Some of the accounts are a part of the lore and tradition of certain areas of the continent, and only by a judicial appraisal may we discriminate between truth and fiction. Other narrations concerning spider bite are woven into the travel history of the various countries, and the material on arachnidism must be deleted before an adjudication is in order. Still other reports are statistical in nature, and because writers of a century or more ago were prone to lack exactitude when quoting figures, these numerical citations of spider bite should be largely discounted. Nevertheless, there is an abundance of evidence tending to show that through the years *Latrodectus* has inflicted her bite upon many persons, resulting in great suffering.

In east, south, and southwest portions of Europe *Latrodectus* thrives. In Greece and neighboring areas she sometimes is known as *L. congoblatus*, in Italy as *falangio de Volterra*. Pliny, of the first century, classified her as one of the *phalangia*. Her most commonly accepted titles, however, are *la malmignatte* and *L. tridecimguttatus*. There are on her underside thirteen triangular or half-moon shaped spots. Reports state that this spider caused the virulent epidemics which occurred in Spain during the years 1833 and 1841. She has a record of bringing suffering to humanity in France, Corsica, Tuscany, and

Sardinia. In the last-named territory, great epidemics occurred in 1833 and again in 1839, when humankind as well as cattle and other domesticated animals fell victim to the bite of this spider.

In 1833 the Royal Academy of Medicine and Surgery at Barcelona appointed Graells, a recognized medical authority of that time, to investigate the effects from the bite of *malmignatte*. Recovery occurred in all of the cases he reported, but, on the other hand, the symptoms were severe. "There was a double puncture, surrounded by red circles, the region of the wound afterwards swelling greatly. The pain and swelling extended over the whole limb, and often to the body, and convulsions occurred, followed by great prostration and collapse."

In southern Russia *Latrodectus* is known to science as *L. lugubris*, and to the native population as *karakurt* (the "black wolf") or Schim. In 1838 and 1839 the nomadic tribes are said to have lost great numbers of cattle through the bite of this species, and it was also reported that there were many human victims. A further statement is that during the season when this spider was most prolific, children and older persons were employed to search the fields and meadows and kill the creatures. They were advised to carry raw onions, and if bitten to rub them upon the wound punctures. This treatment, according to its sponsors, acts as an antidote to the virulent poison.

It was not until 1899, however, that science acknowledged *L. lugubris* as dangerous to humankind. Petrunkevitch tells of an expedition which was sent out that year by the Russian Department of Agriculture, headed by Rossikov, to determine whether or not *karakurt's* bite is poisonous to human beings. Repeatedly the experimenters tried to induce the spider to bite them, but without success. Finally, they concluded that the common belief concerning her dangerous propensities in relation to human beings was erroneous. In this connection, Sczerbina, a member of the expedition, decided to take some pictures. He placed six specimens of *karakurt* on the naked breast of a man, and proceeded with his work. In a flash, however, a black spider ran up the arm of the test object and bit him above the hand. In five minutes the "patient was trembling all over his body, the eyes were dull, the face had an expression of terror. Half an hour later convulsions and cramps set in, accompanied by vomiting, oppressed perspiration and cold sweat. At times the patient became unconscious, and again cried out with pain." Although a doctor arrived within the hour, the cramps continued for an interval of nearly six hours. The succeeding report—which was based upon this and foregoing experiments—lends the suggestion that, while the spider was not always the aggressor, she usually struck with full force when angered.

Reports from Africa indicate the presence of *Latrodectus* in that continent, and mention has been made of the symptoms resulting from her bite. In the northern portion of the continent in Algeria, and on the southern part in South Africa, and to the southeast in Madagascar, this genus of spider has frequently been observed. A number of investigators, beginning as early as 1863, told of this spider in their writings and also recorded case histories. A full description, which mentions also the locations of her web and other biological data together with symptoms noted as resulting from her bite, has been provided. Barrow reports that certain natives dip the points of their arrow heads in a preparation which contains spider poison.

In South Africa prevail three species of *Latrodectus*: *L. geometricus*, *L. concinnus*, and *L. indistinctus*. Her popular name is *knoppie spinnekop*, which, as Villiers points out, in English means "shoe button spider." He states that the first symptoms from its bite "are violent pains and perfectly fantastic perspiring," and that there have been several deaths. Smithers, Finlayson and others describe its appearance, nesting habits, and distribution, and report case histories.

Particular notations have been made of the species inhabiting Madagascar, which is indicated under the names of *mena-vodi* and *vancoho*. Cases have been related in which Negroes were involved, the bite being followed by a condition of syncope which lasted for two days. In that island the belief prevails that the bite of *Latrodectus* will prove fatal unless measures are taken to counteract the poison. These sometimes include cauterizing the wound, but the usual treatment consists of inducing profuse perspiration, and this by means of violent dancing.

Skaife in his reference to the fauna of Africa sums up the situation when he declares that although "the majority of spiders are quite harmless and incapable of inflicting a severe bite, there is one family, known as the deadly spiders, that has a very bad reputation. These spiders are fairly common and may be found lurking in such places as piles of rubbish and outhouses. They are all small, rarely exceeding an inch in length, and they are generally black or brown in color. They may be easily recognized by their very shiny bodies. Several cases have been recorded of severe illness and even death ensuing from the bites of these little creatures. The truth of many of these stories of the deadliness of their bite is doubtful, but they have such a bad reputation in all parts of the world that it seems that there must be some foundation for it, hence it is best to give them a wide berth."

In Asia, *Latrodectus* has been observed, and the official records tell of much suffering from her bite. A report in 1896 concerning a certain area of Russian Central Asia gives statistics in which camels and horses as well as human beings fell victims to the bite of *L. lugubris*, suffered greatly, and, in numerous instances, died. The people of that region, however, have long held the belief—despite the fact that the venom from this spider often proves fatal to human beings—that sheep are immune to her poison. They contend that these animals may eat the spider without experiencing any ill effects, and, in extenuation, that the spider herself has a dislike for the skin of a sheep. Through the years the multitudes have had faith in this legend and when sleeping out of doors always wear sheep skins.

Asia harbors a species of *Latrodectus* called the redback or jockey spider. A typical specimen is colored a soft, velvet black. For her habitat she constructs a web in the sheltered nooks and recesses provided by man-made structures. The red-back spider ranges from Arabia through southern Asia as far as to the Malay Archipelago and Australia. Isolated groups of islands, little known except to the venturesome canoes of the old Polynesian voyagers, have afforded a sanctuary for this spider.

Latrodectus has also been reported in the Hawaiian Islands, and in recent years the identical species which inhabits the United States, *mactans*, has been discovered there. Owing to the fact that it is obviously not a native species, it is probable that the original specimens migrated from one of the Americas, carried thither in an ocean craft. The first of these spiders were discovered in November of 1925 at Koho Head, and later others were found at Waikiki. By the year 1930 the black widow spider had multiplied to such an extent that she has since been recognized as a menace to the pineapple and sugar growers.

At the present time, *Latrodectus* has reached such numerical proportions in Hawaii that efforts have been made to discover her natural enemy and encourage its propagation. One such scheme had its origin in Los Angeles. The newspapers told of a recognized entomologist who sent out a call to householders to collect black widow spider cocoons. He instructed the finders of such to pack them carefully in cotton and send them to him; from the egg sacs he hoped to extract a "pin-head sized wasp," purported to be an antagonist of *Latrodectus*. These were to be shipped to the sugar plantation owners of Hawaii. Whatever merit one might attribute to the plan, it—to say the least—indicated the importance of *mactans* in these islands.

In New Zealand and Australia, *Latrodectus* prevails in great numbers, and more than a score of writers have told of them, listing case histories of victims. The New Zealand species goes under several technical names, including *L. hasseltii* and *L. scelio,* and is known to the natives as *katipo* or the *night stinger.* She is found abundantly within the confines of the beaches and sand dunes, "under logs, tussocks, and driftwood, and especially under the sandbinding pingao or cutty-grass, and in old discarded petrol tins." This spider has created a situation of terror;

the beliefs concerning her are many. One is to the effect that the creature bites only when the moon is in a certain phase; another, that the victim will die if the spider that bit him cannot be found; and yet another, that if the culprit is discovered and burned the patient will recover within three days. It is true that the folklore in the various communities does not agree in minute details; there remains, however, the essential premise that *katipo* is dangerous and should be shunned.

Scientific reports attest to the truth of the tales that are told. Meek, Kellaway, McKay, Lethbridge, Rodway, Frost and others have contributed to the spider literature. The first tells of his son, twenty-three years of age, who was awakened from his sleep by the bite of *katipo*, came into his parent's bed room about an hour afterward and exclaimed, "I am bitten by one of those spiders that the natives have so often spoken to me about, and am full of pain. See, here it is in the bottom of the candlestick." Meek states that he examined the spider, and that her body was about the size of an ordinary pea, and almost black in color. The symptoms experienced during the first twenty-four hours were excruciating pain in the groin, spine, arms, and face. On the second day the pain became intense, and the legs and toes were affected. In a five day period the patient lost twelve pounds of flesh.

Ingram and Musgrave have made extensive studies of arachnidism in Australia. They report that in New South Wales alone there was a total of seven deaths from spider bite over a six-year period, and that one of the spider culprits was *L. hasseltii*. They describe the appearance and habitat of *L. hasseltii*, as well as its distribution, and analyze ninety-eight cases of bites from this creature mentioned in the medical literature of Australia. Sixty-four per cent of the victims were bitten on the genitals while using outdoor toilets, and the others were stricken on the hand, arm, foot, leg, thigh, and head. "Among the 98 cases recorded there are records of six deaths, and an additional death is referred to as having been due to malignant edema following the bite."

The Australian *Latrodectus* is best known under the name of "red-back spider." She constructs a web irregular in form, with guy-lines extending in all directions. Although the creature may be found throughout the continent, she flourishes unabated in the vicinity of Sydney. There the webbed nests may be found in gas meters, gratings of plastered or terra-cotta ventilators placed around the foundations of dwellings, rural out-houses, old rubbish boxes, and empty tins and bottles. In short, she makes her abode in any place she finds convenient for her web.

A number of years ago there was considerable controversy in Australia concerning the effects from the venom of the red-back spider. Some of the observers contended that she was absolutely harmless. McKeown states that there are those who "consider that the Red-back is unjustly accused of its misdeeds, and that it is just another case of giving a dog a bad name. . . ." But he asserts further that he has "never found one of these defenders who was willing to put his opinion to the test—in fact they always treated the spider with a respect equal to, if not greater than, that shown by its detractors."

He describes the effects from the bite of the creature. A tiny red mark usually indicates the site of the puncture. In a typical case, within an hour or so acute nerve pains attack the patient. Accompanying this there is numbness of the limbs, with "tingling sensations like pins and needles" persisting for days. In severe cases there may be partial paralysis, and the victim may also suffer from acute and exhausting shivering fits alternating with profuse sweats, together with nausea and vomiting.

This symptom picture approaches closely that of victims of black widow spider bite in the United States. Indeed, the similarity holds true the world over, for whether it be North or South America, Europe, Africa, or Asia, therein *Latrodectus* may be found, and reliable reports tell of great suffering, and even deaths, resulting from her bite.

5. Early Reported Cases of Spider Bite in the United States *

‸‸

OUR presentation of evidence against the black widow spider of the United States (L. mactans) begins with a recounting of early reported cases of spider bite. In some instances the reports offered few clues other than that an unidentified species of spider was responsible. In other accounts, while the spider was not identified, the symptom picture strikingly resembled that from black widow spider bite. In still other cases a description of the appearance and habits of the spider under investigation left little doubt that she belonged to the species L. mactans, and in some instances the creature was referred to by name.

The first recorded spider bite in America occurred on September 3, 1726, and was described by Dr. Thomas Robie. One Nat Ware of Needham, Massachusetts—upon arising early in the morning, and as he pulled on his stocking—felt something bite his left leg just above the ankle. He crushed the offending agent, which upon examination proved to be a small spider. About half an hour after being bitten he felt a pain in the leg, which in thirty minutes extended to the groin, and also the calf of the left leg.

---

* See Appendix III for tabular listings showing distribution of reported spider-bite cases by states and chronologically.

Pain was experienced in the small of the back approximately an hour later, then in the stomach and right thigh, and afterwards numbness developed in the head. "The pains were not constant and fixed, but erratic and very acute. His pulse was very low and heavy." A doctor in Cambridge was consulted, treatment was given, and the patient recovered.

Comstock in 1803 told of a case that occurred in the month of December two years earlier. A fifteen-year-old girl was visiting upon the Island of Conanicut, Rhode Island, where the weather happened to be remarkably warm. She and another young woman went to a hay stack to procure oat-straw with which to fashion hats to protect them from the sun's rays. As she stooped to cull some straws, a large black spider with "very shiny eyes" ran onto the back of her hand. The girl had heard that such an incident was a good omen, and accordingly permitted the creature to run off on its own accord. As it did so, she felt a slight sensation like the prick of a pin on the back of her hand. That afternoon the affected hand, as well as the arm, began to twitch and pain. The pain gradually shifted to her stomach, increasing in intensity until the morning of the third day, when she became hysterical. She vomited several times on the second and third days, and a physician was called. The girl neglected to tell the doctor about the spider bite; hence he treated her for hysteria. Despite this, however, recovery subsequently took place.

Peter Smith in 1812 mentioned the black widow spider in his *Indian Doctor's Dispensatory*. This famous "Indian Doctor" told of the importance of curing the bite of spiders, especially the *black one* with the *red spot*. Smith mistakenly termed this creature "the tarantula," but, at the same time, spoke with some understanding of the species as being "so common and dreadful in southern climates. . . ." As a treatment he suggested the making of vegetable dye, in the form of mud, by wetting a thimblefull of indigo with good vinegar. This should be applied to the "bite or sting," averred Smith. "If done soon, the danger will be immediately over, and it is stated to me that the place will not swell at all."

Hopton in 1829 reported a spider-bite case, an adult male, that occurred in North Carolina. The symptoms included severe pain in the legs and back, constipation, perspiration, acute urinary retention, nausea, muscle spasms, depression, speech defect, pulse acceleration, delirium, and morbidity. Abbott in 1837 declared that *Latrodectus* was feared in the United States. Stahl in 1838 told of a spider-bite case, a twenty-seven-year-old male, that occurred in Pennsylvania. The symptoms included severe pain in the legs and back, constipation, perspiration, acute urinary retention, vomiting, and morbidity.

James Hall in 1838 told of two deaths from spider bite, but sought to explain them away by declaring that in the first instance there were no physician's reports and that in the second the heat of the day was a deciding factor. He stated that the first death "was occasioned by the bite of a spider, and the belief became current that a peculiarly venomous variety of that reptile existed among us." The second instance was in a man who, while ploughing in the field on a very hot day, was bitten on the arm by a large spider, which he struck and crushed. The alarmed victim ran to his home and sent for a physician, who arrived in about two hours. Shortly thereafter "the patient died."

Hulse in 1839 reported a spider bite case which occurred in Florida. The patient received the bite on the *glans penis*, and experienced severe pain in the abdomen, chest, back, arms, and legs. He manifested anxiety, and the report describes muscle spasms, difficult breathing, and vomiting. In 1841 C. Koch, and in 1842 and 1847, Walckenaer referred in scientific treatises to the black widow.

Hentz in 1850 mentioned the black widow from an arachnological viewpoint, and cited the popular belief concerning the effects of its bite. He described the spider as "deep black, glossy; abdomen with blood-red spots underneath, which sometimes extend above in a chain, and with some waving white lines anteriorly, which are sometimes wanting. . . ." He wrote of its habitat as being "under stones, logs, or clods of earth, where it makes a web, the threads of which are so powerful as to arrest the largest hymenopterous insects, such as bumble-bees." Hentz expressed skepticism concerning the seriousness of its bite, but nevertheless stated that the people in the Southern states believed it to be "very poisonous." He further stated that physicians described its bite as producing "alarming nervous disorders."

Cross in 1859 told of an adult male bitten on the penis in Alabama. He experienced severe pain in the abdomen, muscle spasms, and fever. In 1860, Banks described the case of a five-year-old boy, bitten in Georgia, who developed perspiration, a bluish discoloration of the skin, rigidity, tenderness, and pains in the abdomen, muscle spasms, priapism, local swelling, and fever. The same year Thompson wrote of a thirty-eight-year-old man in Tennessee who experienced not only pain in the abdomen but also in the legs and chest, as well as perspiration, rigidity of the abdomen, delirium, and fever.

Charlotte Taylor, a nature writer of that period, referred to the black widow spider by one of the creature's several scientific names. Although this writer held up to scorn the tales of terror concerning the effects of spider bites, she nevertheless dispensed significant information. In one instance she told of a man in Georgia who, while hunting, was "stung" by a black widow spider. Accordingly he "gave away his watch, bade his friends goodbye and made every preparation for an early demise." And while the anticipated consequence did not materialize, the incident reveals the fear with which the black widow spider was regarded even at that early date.

Semple in 1875 reported five cases of spider bites in Virginia; the outstanding symptoms were severe pain in the chest, back, and arms, and nausea, vomiting, and dyspnoea. Grinnel in 1876 wrote of a case in what was then called the Indian Territory. Tomkins wrote in 1884 of a case in West Virginia, the patient being an adult female. The symptoms from the bite were severe pain in the abdomen and legs, and nausea, vomiting, and muscle spasms. In addition there were local swelling, insomnia, speech defect, restlessness and delirium.

While these early case histories clearly reveal the fact that throughout many decades persons in the United States have experienced bites from the black widow spider, they nevertheless do not indicate the vast number of instances of suffering brought about by the venom of this creature. In all probability only a comparatively few of the actual cases of black widow spider bite were recorded. During the early years the medical profession was unfamiliar with symptoms of arachnidism; hence it is most likely that in numerous instances wherein human beings were bitten by members of the species *L. mactans*, the resulting suffering was diagnosed not as spider bite but as some other disease. Furthermore, in the frontier life then dominant, a large portion of the people were administered to by poorly trained physicians—or none at all. Even so, the spider-bite cases reported during the pioneer days hold an interest from both historical and clinical viewpoints.

6. Investigating Latrodectus Mactans

wwwwwwwwwwwwwwwwwwwwwwwwwwwwwwwwwwwwwwwwwwwwwwwwwwwwwwwwwwwwwwww

THE FIRST comprehensive investigation of the spider-bite question in the United States was reported by Riley and Howard in *Insect Life*, a periodical bulletin which was issued by the United States Department of Agriculture, and which appeared from 1888 to 1895. The editors made their initial report in the January, 1889, issue under the title, "A Contribution to the Literature of Fatal Spider Bites."

They at the outset candidly admitted that in the cases reported up to that time "the spider has seldom if ever been seen by a reliable observer to inflict the wound. . . ." The reports were unconvincing, repeated experiments testing spider venom on man and animals had been unsuccessful, and the unfounded claims had to be rejected. Sufficient evidence of the relationship of bites to symptoms and experimental verification were needed before the nature of the spider poisoning could be recognized, just as similar studies were needed to establish the causes of other diseases. In addition to this, they were aware that among the people at large the impression prevailed that fatal spider bites occurred with frequency, and that, on the other hand, most of their fellow scientists of that day doubted the existence, in the United States, of any spider

54

the bite of which in itself could cause a serious train of symptoms in a normal body. Still, despite these limitations as to the evidence, and notwithstanding the contradictory beliefs that were held, they felt that the available material warranted a consideration and a conclusion.

With this in mind, they reviewed selected portions of the literature and recounted case histories. Attention was called to the fact that in the alleged spider bites throughout the years, one genus of spiders, *Latrodectus*, was more closely involved than any other. Because species of this genus occur in such widely distant localities as south Europe, the southern United States (until recent times the black widow spider was mistakenly thought to be absent in the North) and New Zealand, together with the fact that they "are uniformly set aside by the natives as poisonous, when there is nothing especially dangerous in their appearance," Riley and Howard declared that it "must at least be admitted that certain spiders of the genus *Latrodectus* have the power to inflict poisonous bites, which may (probably exceptionally and depending upon exceptional conditions) bring about the death of a human being."

Following publication of the issue of *Insect Life* containing this paper, many communications were received recording cases which substantiated the authors' conclusions. Reports came from North Carolina and Georgia, California and Illinois, Ohio and Delaware, Ceylon, Madagascar, New Zealand, Australia, Mexico, and Jamaica. Sometimes the writers told of hearsay evidence and voiced their opinion therefrom. At other times the correspondents depicted the symptom picture in patients as they themselves had witnessed it, but without a description of the spider that had inflicted the damage. At other times, however, the culprit was seen and the symptoms recorded. Taken as a whole, the data was sufficient to isolate and brand as dangerous the species belonging to the genus *Latrodectus*.

That Riley and Howard approached the study with an unbiased attitude, passing on to the readers the information received without prejudicial censoring, is evidenced by the fact that some of the testimony was contrary to their own belief. Subsequent observations have proved that they, and not the correspondents, were wrong. One of the letters was from Dr. C. R. Corson, who recounted at length a series of case histories. He mentioned that the spider responsible for the injury to the patients inhabited outdoor privies. Riley and Howard had not hitherto associated *L. mactans* with such a habitat, and they accordingly looked askance at this statement. The suggestion forwarded was that the spider in question could belong either to one of the genera *Amaurobius* or *Caelotes*, or possibly to *Tegenaria*, *Pholcus*, or *Dictyna*. But a fresh communication from a writer who had spent some days in a certain county in Georgia caused them to modify their surmise. The correspondent shipped to the editors specimens of a spider which he had captured in an irregularly spun web several inches below the level of the seat in a privy. Riley and Howard promptly identified them as individuals of the species *mactans*, and asserted that "in view of this direct evidence," it seemed likely that at least in some of the cases described by Dr. Corson the privy-inhabiting species involved was *L. mactans*.

The symptoms of the cases reported by Dr. Corson and others tally strikingly with those recorded today. Corson

told of six cases, all of which centered in the abdomen
and back, with restlessness, perspiration, muscle spasms,
anxiety, elevated temperature, accelerated pulse, and delirium. Wright of California sent, in a glass tube, a specimen of *Latrodectus*, or "poisonous spider," to the editors.
He stated that he personally knew "two people (one of
them a lady) who were bitten, presumably by this species
of spider, while in privies, and both persons were seriously ill for weeks. . . ." Smith chronicles a case from
Virginia, in a male, and among the symptoms which he
listed was a local lesion. Eaton told of fatal cases in California; Wight mentioned twelve cases with one death; and
Blanchard gave evidence bearing on spider bite.

In detail, the cases communicated to Riley and Howard
possessed much human interest. A Negro field hand experienced a bite—probably from the species *mactans*—on
the ankle as he rested near a spring of water. He spat
tobacco juice on the "sting" and soon felt no pain. An
hour or so afterward, however, various pains racked his
body. He attempted to ride to his dwelling, but while en
route fell off his horse in an unconscious state. Agonizing
spasms of pain endured for several days, and it was not
until two months afterward that he was able to do any
work. A white man was bitten on the *glans penis* while in
a privy. Though a "muscular" man, he was bed-ridden for
two days, and the symptoms manifested were restlessness,
anxiety, and tetanic contractions, together with severe
lancinating pains in the abdomen and back.

There are other cases which, because of the startling
manner in which the spiders found lodgment on their
respective victims, deserve narration. In one a "black
spider with a red spot on it" crawled onto an adult male's

neck, and as he attempted to brush her off, delivered a severe bite. In another, a man while putting on his sock was bitten "by a spider which had a red spot on the abdomen." He experienced much agonizing pain, but recovered. Another concerned a Negro woman; a spider dropped from the ceiling and bit her on the face as she lay in bed. Edema was a symptom, together with severe pains which lasted for several days.

Still another instance was told of an infant, who about ten o'clock at night startled its parents by "piercing cries." For some moments the father and mother were perplexed as to the nature of the infant's trouble. Finally the mother, as she coddled the little one, (who was sitting up in its cradle and suffering from fright and great pain), observed that the underlid of its eye was highly inflamed. The swelling increased and extended to the side of the nose and cheek, high fever set in, the skin became dry and hot, and the pulse rapid but very weak. Only after the third day was there promise of recovery, and the cause of the trouble was not revealed until the parents—upon locating the seat of the pain—discovered a spider on the baby's pillow. This the father captured and placed in a pill box. Riley and Howard later received the spider and identified her as *L. mactans.*

There is, finally, the fatal case reported by John Dick of Greensboro, North Carolina. An employee on his farm, "in perfect health," was bitten by a spider identified as a black widow about eight-thirty in the morning, and died between ten and eleven o'clock that night. "Small pimples were raised in the neighborhood of the bite, but no puncture was discernible. Intermittent pains and spasms ended in a comatose condition from which he did not rally."

Little wonder is it that Riley and Howard reached a conclusion regarding *L. mactans* and the effect of her bite upon man. In the March, 1892, issue of *Insect Life* (after three years of receiving numerous communications from persons the world over), they—in reply to a correspondent —asserted that there "is no doubt that the spiders of this genus *Latrodectus* are very poisonous and that their bite has been followed by severe illness *and in some cases death.*"

7. Cumulative Medical Reports

~~~~~~

DURING and following Riley and Howard's publications in *Insect Life*, reports continued to appear elsewhere concerning spider-bite cases. In 1889 Wade cited a case from California in which the spider responsible for the injury had her nest in an outdoor privy. The patient, an adult, was bitten "on the most dependent part of the scrotum." Wade saw the victim twelve hours after the incident, and at that time he was restless, incoherent in speech, and wet with cold perspiration. The first night he was delirious and "had pain in the back and legs, numbness, tingling of hands and feet, and a sense of constriction around the chest, so that breathing was laborious." Although the man ultimately recovered, for at least another week he continued to complain of aching and weakness of legs. In 1891 Smith reported a case from Virginia in which the victim was a male, and the symptom mentioned was local edema. In 1892 Duffield told of an Alabama case in which the spider culprit was found in a privy. The patient, twenty-two years old, was bitten on the penis. He experienced severe pain in the back, and other symptoms noted were acute urinary retention, rigid abdomen, muscle spasm, priapism, and speech defect. In the same year Wilson noted local lesions from spider bites.

In 1895, Brown listed sixteen cases from California. In describing the type of spider responsible for the suffering he stated that "It is about· one half an inch in length with long legs. It has a small cephalothorax and a large abdomen. It is glossy black, with a red spot on its underside. It is not hairy or fuzzy, its abdomen appearing like a hard glossy black shell. . . ." Included among the symptoms in his sixteen spider-bite cases were severe pain in the abdomen, legs, and chest, and painful breathing, perspiration, rigid and tender abdomen, depression, anxiety, and a morbid condition. With reference to L. mactans, Brown declared that "there seems no doubt that this little animal is provided with a venom that for its size and the quantity of the poison, far exceeds that of any other living thing."

In 1896, Schenck reported a case of spider bite with local lesion, Presley listed nine cases from Texas, and Peck told of an adult female from that state who felt pain throughout her body, with restlessness, acute urinary retention, muscle spasms, anxiety, and a temperature of 101 degrees following a spider bite. In 1897 Riddick described a case from North Carolina in which the victim, a forty-year-old male, experienced severe pain in the abdomen, legs, chest, back, and arms, and there were restlessness, rigid and tender abdomen, muscle spasms, and a temperature of 102 degrees.

In 1901, Browning, noted tuberculosis specialist and naturalist, prepared a paper in which he cited Professor A. J. Cook of Pomona College, California, and depicted some of the spider's habits. He described the construction of her nest by summing it up as "a large open web void of geometrical symmetry." He sent letters of inquiry to various physicians, and from the replies was able to list seventy patients as being victims of the bite of that number of "little black spiders." The habitat of *Latrodectus* was frequently reported as the "outdoor privy." The site of the bite in a goodly portion of male patients was on the penis. Included among the symptoms mentioned were severe pain in the abdomen, legs, chest, and back, together with nausea, constipation, restlessness, perspiration, acute urinary retention, muscle spasms, depression, anxiety, and local edema.

Browning's contribution included in detail a fatal case which took place in the practice of Dr. George C. Clark of Fullerton, California. On July 26, 1900, about 1:15 P.M., Clark was called by an adult patient, who said that while in an outhouse a few minutes before he had been bitten on the penis by a spider. Clark hastened to the bedside of the victim, who was suffering great pain at the site of the bite. Although there were no visible fang marks, the examination revealed "a mottled appearance of the glans and prepuce. . . ." Among the symptoms were severe pain in the abdomen, legs, and back, and there was difficult breathing, restlessness, cyanosis, muscle spasms, anxiety, a temperature of 105 degrees, and delirium. In his suffering he "would be in a chair, then on the bed, then on the floor, and so on over and over again." From the beginning the patient seemed thoroughly possessed with the idea that he was fatally bitten and would die. And despite various treatments, death did occur at three o'clock A.M., which was approximately thirteen hours and forty-five minutes from the time of the incident. The next day the water closet was turned over, and the investigators discovered three or four black, medium-sized spiders with reddish spots.

In 1903, Worcester listed four cases from Florida. The symptoms mentioned were severe pain in the abdomen and legs, and there were vomiting, constipation, rigid abdomen, muscle spasms, and evidence of a rise in temperature. In 1904 Sharp described spider-bite symptoms. In 1907 Hodgdon reported a case from Maryland in which the patient, a male, experienced severe pain throughout his body. In 1915 Coleman listed an instance in California due to a specimen of L. mactans that inhabited a privy. The patient, an adult, was bitten on the penis. The symptoms were severe pain in the abdomen, legs, and chest, and constipation, difficulty of breathing, cyanosis, muscle spasms, local edema, insomnia, and a temperature of 100 degrees.

In 1921, Reese described two cases of spider bite, one of which was fatal. The fatal case occurred in Oklahoma, in the summer of 1920. The site of the bite was on the penis. The victim, a strong healthy man of thirty-eight, felt something like a pin stick him but did not look until bitten again. He then discovered the black widow spider, which he killed. A doctor was called, and later, two others. When the first arrived, the patient was in great agony and could not lie still. "The pain traveled up the penis through the cords to one group of muscles and another, shifting about all the time." Various treatments were administered, but he died about thirty-two hours after the bite.

In 1921 Kennedy listed three cases from Florida, all adults. Included among the symptoms were severe generalized pain, painful breathing, and a slight rise in temperature. In 1922 Woody told of a case in Virginia in which the spider occupied a webbed nest in a privy. The patient, sixty-two years old, was bitten on the penis, and the symptoms experienced were severe pain in the abdomen, legs, and back, and constipation, perspiration, acute urinary retention, cyanosis, and rigid abdomen. In the same year Watson described four male cases from Florida in which the spider in each instance inhabited a privy. Each of the victims was bitten on the penis. They "suffered intense pain, accompanied by severe abdominal disturbances, convulsions and delirium. In one case the abdominal pain was so intense and pronounced that the patient who had been sent to a hospital in a distant city was, upon arrival, promptly operated on for appendicitis." Although all four patients ultimately recovered, the "severe symptoms lasted from 24 hours in one to over a week in another. In one case the physician reported four days after the patient had been bitten that he was not yet out of danger." In his conclusion regarding *L. mactans*, Watson asserts that "these experiences would indicate that the bite of this species, at least when administered in a tender part of the body, is very serious, exceedingly painful, and even dangerous."

In 1924, a Dr. Caldwell was reported to have died in Kansas from blood poisoning following a spider bite. In that year Brown listed a case from Texas; in the same year Gallagher told of one from the same state; and in 1925 Rulison reported another from California. In these three accounts, the spiders involved had their webs in privies. All three victims were adults who were bitten on the penis. In Brown's case, the symptoms were severe pain in the abdomen, legs, and back, and vomiting, constipation, restlessness, perspiration, muscle spasms, and anxiety. In the case cited by Gallagher, there was severe pain in the legs, chest, and back. In Rulison's case, the patient had severe pain in the abdomen, vomiting, perspiration, cyanosis, rigid abdomen, and depression.

In summarizing, we note that from 1889 to 1925 there were from independent sources numerous accounts of black widow spider bite, with several deaths resulting. Two of the fatalities, those depicted by Clark and Reese, are related in detail. The habitat of the black widow spider was mentioned most frequently as being the outdoor toilet. Severe systemic pain, rigid abdomen, and perspiration were listed prominently as symptoms. Special recognition must be given the paper of C. C. Browning, for it marks an epoch in the history of spider-bite poisoning as the first extensive collection of cases.

8. *Spider Bite as a Clinical Entity* *

IN 1926 Emil Bogen, then a resident physician at the Los Angeles General Hospital, submitted a paper on "Arachnidism (Spider Poisoning)" which was awarded the California Medical Association Prize for that year. These studies mark another epoch, not only because they present actual scientific material, but especially because it is from this time that the medical profession, and naturalists in general, have recognized spider-bite poisoning as a clinical entity. This was due to the large amount of evidence collected, and to the fact that the material was widely publicized, being presented before several sections of the California and the American Medical Associations. It was published in the *Journal of the American Medical Association*, reaching practically the entire profession. Further publication in *California and Western Medicine* and in the *Archives of Internal Medicine* brought it particularly before the local groups and the specialists. A motion picture of the black widow spider shown at the conventions and the wide newspaper publicity then received also aided in establishing general recognition of the facts set forth.

---

* See Appendices I and II for supplementary case histories of victims of the black widow spider.

Bogen's report not only summarized fifteen spider-bite cases cared for at the Los Angeles General Hospital, but also reviewed all the available literature on the subject. The Los Angeles cases were all males, ranging in age from two to sixty-five years, of whom more than half were young adults. Five were Mexican, one Negro, two foreign born, and the other seven native whites. Six were common laborers, eight skilled workers, and one was an infant. Five of the bites occurred within the city of Los Angeles, the other ten in the suburbs. Most of them occurred in the evening or early morning of the summer or early autumn. Thus, five occurred between 8:00 and 9:00, and four between 9:00 and 12:00 P.M.; one occurred at 3:00, and four between 8:00 and 11:00 A.M. There was one instance each in April, May, and October, but two patients were bitten in June, five in July, two in August, and three in September. "The spider was located in a toilet in eleven instances, in a factory once, and in bed once. Most of the patients had seen the actual spider, which they described as black and shiny, and several mentioned a red spot on its belly.

"The bite occurred on the penis in ten patients, the scrotum in two, the back in two, and the abdomen in one. Local signs consisting of one or two tiny pink or red spots were found at the site in eight cases, and local symptoms in that region, after the first momentary prick, were complained of in five. The chief symptom—in every instance—was pain. This was described by seven patients as severe; by three patients each as continuous or aching; by two patients each as sharp, dull, stinging cramping, or doubling up, and by others as considerable, great, burning, throbbing, cutting, tingling, shooting, rheumatic or generalized." The pain was located in the legs in eleven cases and in the abdomen in nine, but was also present in the chest, back, arms, and penis in five cases each, in the groin in three cases, and all over in four.

"Perspiration, restlessness and vomiting were complained of by seven patients; constipation by six; nausea by four; difficulty in breathing by three; dizziness, chills, urinary retention, incoordination and edema of the face and of the legs by two, and hiccough, thirst and cough by one patient each." Thirteen patients appeared to be in agony on admission; cyanosis was seen in five; the pupils were dilated in two, were small in one and irregular in one, and a heart murmur was heard in one. The abdomen was rigid in twelve patients, but tender in only three. The knee jerk and other reflexes were overactive in seven cases; tremors and twitching were found in four, and priapism was noted in one.

The pain appeared immediately in six cases and within a quarter of an hour in six others. It reached the maximum severity within a quarter of an hour in three cases, in an hour in five cases, in two hours in three cases, and in four hours in two. "Three patients were seen at the hospital within two hours after the bite; four within six hours; five within twelve hours, and the others within forty-eight hours. The diagnosis was not made definitely at the time of admission in the first five cases admitted, perhaps because we were not then familiar with the condition, for there has been no hesitancy in recognizing the last ten cases, eight of which occurred within the year 1925. The differential diagnosis included infection following insect bite, an acute surgical abdominal condition such as ruptured gastric ulcer or acute appendicitis with peritonitis, renal colic, food poisoning and lobar pneumonia.

"Eight patients had a subnormal temperature at the time of admission, but in nearly all a mild fever developed during their hospital stay, in six instances reaching 100° F. or more, but in no case going over 101° F. The pulse was generally retarded as compared with the temperature, being below 72° in half the patients on admission and falling below 66° in the majority during their first few days in the hospital. The respiratory rate was generally slightly accelerated on admission, but soon came down to 20, which was the average rate during the remainder of their stay in the hospital." Two patients had urinary retention requiring catheterization on the day of the bite, and almost all were constipated, enduring one day, and in six cases, two days without a bowel movement.

Hypertension was found in each patient examined, the blood pressure averaging 150 systolic over 87 diastolic on admission. Repeated readings, however, showed a rapid drop, the systolic averaging only 136 on the day after admission. "Urinalysis showed a trace of albumen in three cases, with hyaline or granular casts in four, pus cells in three, and indican and blood in one case each. Stool examination revealed blood in one case. The Wassermann test was four plus in two cases, two plus in one, suspicious once and negative eight times. Leukocytosis was present in almost every case, averaging 14,761 in the nine cases examined on the day of admission, 11,600 in the five cases examined on the second day, 10,720 in the four cases examined on the third day in the hospital, the highest count being 21,000 on admission, and the lowest 5,900 several days after the bite. There generally was a relative polymorphonuclear leukocytosis, averaging 80 per cent in the eight cases recorded. The red blood cell count was not constant, averaging 5,000,000 on the seven cases recorded, with an average hemoglobin estimation of about 85 per cent. Altogether more than sixty physicians saw these patients while they were in the hospital."

In the second phase of Bogen's study (a review of the literature) he found that during the century preceding 1926 more than 150 cases of poisonous spider bites had been reported by thirty-three physicians in the United States. Although two-thirds of these occurred in California, the remainder were scattered over more than a dozen states. "More than 80 per cent of the victims were males, and the majority were bitten on the penis or adjacent parts while sitting in an outdoor toilet; others on the hands, feet or other exposed parts. All ages have been reported. A minister and a college professor have not been spared, but most of the victims were farmers or rural laborers, as might be expected from the habitat of the spider. Most of the bites occurred either in the early morning or in the evening in the summer or autumn, but this was not the invariable rule, as cases have been known in almost every month of the year. The spider actually responsible for the bite was captured and identified by arachologists in about a dozen cases, but usually it was described as a *shiny black spider*, and the *red spot* on the abdomen was frequently mentioned.

"A stinging or sticking sensation was noted at first, but this soon disappeared, and except for a tiny red spot sometimes seen, there was no mark or swelling to indicate the location of the bite. In less than half an hour, however, the characteristic pain appeared, increasing in severity for several hours. It has been vividly described as intense, violent, agonizing, exquisite, excruciating, griping, cramping, shooting, lancinating, aching and numbing, and was either continuous and incessant or paroxysmal and intermittent. It was felt in the abdomen and generally also in the legs, back, chest and 'all over'; less often in the head, shoulders and arms. The pain spreads from the site of the wound by continuity; thus, the patients bitten on the penis usually have pain in the groin and then in the abdomen, while those bitten on the wrist have pain in the arm and then in the chest before it reaches the abdomen, suggesting that the venom spreads by the lymphatics and acts in the muscles rather than in the central nervous system." The final distribution of the pain, disregarding the order of development, however, appears to be fairly uniform, irrespective of the site of the initial lesion, and the pain in the abdomen and legs follows bites on the wrist or back just as regularly as it does those on the penis or ankle.

"In addition to the acute pain, which was evidenced in most cases by writhing, rolling, doubling up, muscle spasms and paroxysmal contractions, many other symptoms were described. The most common, in the order of frequency, includes profuse cold sweats, restlessness, anxiety, difficulty in breathing, anorexia, nausea and vomiting, constipation, cyanosis, delirium, prostration, shock, insomnia, speech disturbances and acute urinary retention. Tremors, twitching, paralyses, convulsions, localized swelling of the bitten part or of other tissues, chills, dizziness, priapism, jaundice and a macular skin eruption were also encountered.

"An extreme boardlike rigidity of the abdomen was the most striking physical finding, but abdominal tenderness was rarely mentioned. Circulatory disturbances, evidenced by cyanosis and an unduly slow or rapid pulse, were often noted, but actual figures were lacking. The patients were usually seen by the physician within a few hours after the bite, but the diagnosis was not always made at once, and in several instances the patient was operated on by mistake for an acute appendicitis or other acute surgical abdominal disease, while biliary or renal colic, acute pancreatitis, ruptured gastric ulcer and various forms of poisoning were suggested in others. The most acute symptoms lasted a number of hours, no relief being felt for more than six hours in half the cases reported. The pain then generally subsided in from twelve to forty-eight hours after the onset, but complete ease was often not secured for more than a week, and many complained of weakness and recurring pains for many weeks thereafter."

Upon the evidence obtained at the Los Angeles General Hospital, together with a review of the literature, Bogen concludes that "the acceptance of arachnidism, or spider bite poisoning as a true clinical entity in the field of general medicine" is warranted.

In 1932 and again in 1935, Bogen made other reports concerning the black widow spider. In the first, he stated that since his 1926 paper, the total number of cases of arachnidism treated at the Los Angeles General Hospital, beginning with the year 1915, had increased to sixty. "Most of the patients were men, but seven, or twelve percent, were females. The ages ranged from one to seventy-two years, but the majority were young adults. The majority were native white Americans, but seventeen Mexicans and five Orientals were included. Nearly half of the patients were common laborers, but six housewives, nine children, and more than a score of skilled workers, including a sheriff, a painter and a teacher were affected.

"Most of the bites occurred in the more sparsely settled districts, the majority of them being outside of the city limits of Los Angeles, but instances were noted in the more crowded neighborhoods also. The bites took place, for the most part, in the evening or early morning in summer or autumn. The spider was seen and described in the majority of instances, but a number of cases were diagnosed from the characteristic clinical picture alone, often confirmed thereafter by a successful search of the premises for the spider.

"The culprit was variously described as large, medium sized or small, but always as *black*, and *smooth* or *shiny*, and usually as being marked with red on the abdomen, especially on the ventral side, where the *hourglass shape* of the *red mark* was often noted. Many of the spiders, alive or dead, were brought in for recognition." They were located in privies in half of the cases, but in this series there were ten patients who were bitten while in their own homes, most of them while in bed. Several .cases originated in automobiles or garages, and in several the spider was found in clothes which had been hanging in exposed places—porches, garages, and yards.

"The site of the bite was on the penis or neighboring structures in half of the cases, but the extremities were bitten in sixteen instances, the body ten times and the head twice. This is a much higher incidence of extragenital localization than has been previously reported, due to the fact that the spiders in the more recent cases have been found more often in situations other than the classical one beneath the seat of a privy."

In addition to his comments regarding the Los Angeles General Hospital cases, Bogen states that during the five years since his work was first issued (1926) more than a dozen different authors had published accounts of over seventy-five additional cases of arachnidism in the United States, and that, moreover, by personal communications there had been revealed more than a hundred other cases hitherto unpublished. From the early years through the nineteenth century and on down to 1932, Bogen listed 380 cases of poisonous spider bite cases, with seventeen deaths, which took place in eighteen states.

As to the sum total of unreported cases which have occurred during the history of the United States, no figures can possibly be obtained, since physicians formerly lacked knowledge regarding the symptoms of spider bite. Owing to this professional ignorance they have undoubtedly failed to record a great many cases. Bogen in his 1932 report, in speaking of arachnidism, states that "in view of the fact that nineteen instances of this condition were seen at a single hospital in Los Angles during the past year, it appears probable that the true incidence of the disease throughout the country annually exceeds hundreds, and possibly thousands, of cases."

In his 1935 paper, prepared in collaboration with Russell N. Loomis, Bogen declared that since 1926 there had been published more than a score of articles annually on the spider bite theme, and that this had "undoubtedly contributed much to awaken the medical profession to the possibilities of diagnosis of this condition." In addition he stated that since 1932 more than two hundred cases had been tabulated by thirty different writers. This brought the total number of recorded spider-bite cases in the history of the United States up to 615, with thirty-eight deaths. This data was calculated from 130 reports. By the year 1935 the black widow spider had been reported in forty-three states; persons had been treated for spider bite in twenty-four states with deaths resulting in eight. Bogen further states that several deaths from the bite of the black widow spider "are now being listed annually in one state alone, and no part of our country appears to be entirely free from this dangerous creature."

In 1942, Bogen pointed out that the rarity of fatal outcome from black widow spider bite should not be overlooked. "The fascination of monstrosity, the dramatic symptomatology of the condition, and the great prominence accorded the spider in recent years by the public press and other agencies should not mislead us into overemphasizing its importance. Arachnidism, like hydrophobia and rattlesnake bite, kills a small number of Americans each year, but cannot be compared, in importance, with diseases like tuberculosis, diphtheria, typhoid fever or smallpox. Spider bite is also preventable, however, and so efforts to increase recognition of its danger and to explain means of avoiding it are to be encouraged.

"In view of the wide dissemination of this species, it is surprising that spider bites are as infrequent as appears to be the case. Moreover, the fatality rate, that is, the frequency of death among those bitten, is quite low. Published figures show about five deaths in every hundred cases of arachnidism treated, but these are almost certainly excessive. Non-fatal cases remain unreported more often than fatal ones, many persons bitten by the spider do not receive medical treatment, and some do not even develop symptoms of poisoning.

"Most of the deaths from black widow spider bite which have been reported seem to be due to some complication of the bite, rather than to lethal potency of the venom itself. In a few cases, where excessive dosage of the venom were received, as in bites of infants or small children, or where multiple bites were received by the same individual from several spiders at the same time, the fatality may have been caused by direct effect of the poison.

"More common are the deaths among elderly individuals, with impaired circulatory system, which, under the stress of the muscle spasms and increased blood pressure resulting from the poison, produced a fatal cerebral hemorrhage or apopletic stroke.

"Also common are infections of various kinds, gaining entrance through the portal of entry afforded by the bite of a creature notorious for living in unclean surroundings. Tetanus, erysipelas, and hemolytic streptococcus septicemia have all been reported responsible for deaths following spider bites.

"Misguided treatment itself has been responsible for some of the deaths recorded. Ill advised therapeutic administrations of alcoholic potions have been blamed for fatal outcome in some cases. Abdominal operations, performed under mistaken diagnoses, even despite a definite history of spider-bite poisoning, preceded some of the deaths. Perusal of the records of some of the other patients who survived makes one wonder how they resisted the treatment so heroically.

"Whatever the frequency, or the exact mechanism of death, however, the fact remains that people do die after spider bites, and that preventive measures against arachnidism are therefore potentially lifesaving."

9. Experiments with Latrodectus on Animals

wwwwwwwwwwwwwwwwwwwwwwwwwwwwwwwwwwwwwwwwwwwwwwwwwwwwwwwwwwwwwwwwwww

TO DETERMINE the potential toxic qualities of *Latro-dectus*, many persons have tested this spider's venom on animals. The experiments upon various animals, although conducted in each of the five continents, have in the main been carried on in the Americas. During the eighteenth century, however, Baghlivi, Serrao, Toti, Marmocchi, and others made testings with *L. tridecimguttatus*. Breeger in 1888 asserted that the poison of *L. karakurt*, the "black wolf" of Russia, was sufficient—even when introduced in small doses—to cause death in warm-blooded animals. In 1889 Frost reported death resulting in one rat and severe symptoms in another from bites of *L. scelio*, the Australian *katipo*, and mentioned a dog as practically unaffected.

In 1901 Professor Kobert experimented with *L. kara-kurt*. Taking the fore parts from the bodies of eight specimens, he mixed the materials in a physiological solution of salt. After permitting the mixture to stand for an hour, he cleansed it by the addition of water, drop for drop, for twenty-four hours. Three cubic centimeters of this extract, upon being injected into the jugular vein of a cat weighing 2,450 grams, caused the animal to become paralyzed and lie in whatever position it was placed. The sensibility of the skin of the extremities and the rump was so reduced that there was no reaction from cutting and sticking. There quickly followed dyspnoea, convulsions, and paralysis of the respiratory muscles and the heart. Within twenty-eight minutes the creature was dead. In 1902 Kobert reported that a similar extract was highly hemolytic and poisonous also to dogs. About this time Sachs, in Ehrlich's laboratory, reported an extensive series of experiments showing that an extract of the common garden spider also contains a powerful hemolysin. In 1914 Castelli of Italy stated that an extract from *L. tridecimguttatus* injected in rabbits and guinea pigs produced death very quickly.

In continental United States testings of *L. mactans* on animals have been numerous. Kellogg in 1915 reported experiments by Coleman, who dissected the poison glands of a matured black widow spider, macerated the virus in ten drops of distilled water, and injected it subcutaneously into the abdomen of an eight-months-old cat. In about five minutes a series of convulsions of the clonic type set in, to be quickly followed by a tonic spasm, and within ten minutes the cat died. Additional experiments were made in which spider venom was injected into cats and also into a rabbit. Death to the animal followed in each case. Coleman further reported testings in which macerated eggs of the black widow spider were used, and injections brought death to a cat but produced no marked effect in a dog.

In 1922 Baerg experimented with white rats. In one test two animals about four weeks old were used, and, as a preparation for the test, the hairs on the inside of the left hind leg were clipped off. Two matured female black widow spiders were induced to bite the prepared part of the rat's leg. The fangs remained inserted for several seconds. Shortly both rats humped up, turned their heads underneath until their faces rested on the floor of the cage, and, from time to time, jerked forward as if in convulsions. Their eyes were usually closed, and when they essayed to walk it was in an unsteady and stumbling gait. It was from six to ten hours before recovery took place and normal behavior was resumed. Additional experiments indicated that in rats immunity may be developed.

In 1926 Bogen reported spider-poison experiments on warm blooded animals. Repeated injections of macerated suspensions of L. mactans, as well as solution of the expressed poison glands, were made without noticeable effects in a number of creatures, including rabbits, chickens, cats, and white rats. In contrast to this was a further experiment in which a specimen of L. mactans was applied to the penis of a young male rat until it took a firm bite. The rat squealed, and a few minutes later it arched its back in a sort of hump and appeared to become dejected and depressed. The following day motion pictures were made which demonstrated its almost paralytic gait, its humped back and its sluggish behavior. Two days later it was found dead in its cage, partly eaten by the other rats.

In 1932 Bogen reported further experimental work with the spider and with extracts from her poison glands. These tests—for the most part—confirmed his findings of six years before. The bite of the spider produced marked and sometimes fatal symptoms in mice as well as in rats in many, but not all, of the experiments performed. No consistent effect was obtained, however, by the injection of the macerated extracts of the whole spider or its glands alone into mice, rats, guinea pigs, rabbits, cats, or chickens.

In 1926 Larsen told of experiments with specimens of *L. mactans* in the Hawaiian Islands. The experimenters captured a specimen in its natural habitat, and after allowing it to become acclimated to the laboratory, they exposed several guinea pigs and two rabbits to its tender mercies. The animals were bitten on the nose and ear. Within ten minutes the first muscular twitchings began to appear. These continued at rapid intervals, first one part of the body and then the other being affected. The animals frequently leaped almost from the floor, and froth covered their mouths. The hind legs were sometimes affected and seemed to be partly paralyzed. Within half an hour, the creatures fell over on their sides in a semiconscious condition, and it was from four to six hours before recovery was completed.

In 1932 Hall and Vogelsang published their experiments with *L. mactans*. Twenty-five matured black widow spiders were used in the experiments, which were conducted with guinea pigs. The animals usually evidenced pain at the time of the bite by flinching or squealing. The symptoms included a rigid tender abdomen, a sitting position, hunched up with back arched and fur ruffled, strong, spasmodic, and uncontrollable contractions of the legs (which often dashed the animal into the wall or would have thrown it off the table if not protected, and which from its inception increased in intensity), and the development of difficult and noisy respirations, which in the severe cases went on rapidly to a pulmonary edema.

Tissues of the animals which died one to five hours after being bitten showed no significant pathology other than the pulmonary edema mentioned. Those that died after forty-eight hours, however, revealed numerous areas of necrosis and hemorrhages of the liver, and rare areas in the kidney, spleen, and adrenals. Following recovery from the bites, subsequent attacks caused no symptoms other than local sloughs which developed in twenty-four hours and crushed and healed within a week.

In 1933 and 1934 Herms, Bailey, and McIvor experimented with black widow spiders, using rats in one series. The creatures showed nervousness upon being bitten; they scratched the floor of the cage and ran aimlessly about, at the same time sneezing and scratching their bodies. When sleeping, their heads were drawn under their bodies, resting on the floor. By the morning of the second day the animals were normal.

Guinea pigs proved more susceptible than rats to the spider venom, as was proved in further experiments. Animals of various ages were used, and the spiders employed were adult female *L. mactans*. Some were matrons with no family experience, but others had spun cocoons and reared families. The experiments showed that the venom killed guinea pigs weighing from 250 to 500 grams in intervals of from one and three quarters to four hours.

The experimenters further permitted a black widow spider to bite three different guinea pigs in succession at intervals of one hour, with the result that the first animal died in less than two hours; the second became ill, but recovered in two days; and the third showed no reaction to the bite except an occasional sneeze during the first twenty-four hours following the bite. As a further test, one week after the first bite the second animal was again sacrificed to the black widow spider and showed no symptoms of illness, and a month later the same animal was bitten a third time, registering only a slight reaction to the venom.

In 1934 Blair reported certain conclusions from his experimental studies. He stated that mice, rats, guinea pigs, and chickens exhibited marked reactions to the venom of *L. mactans*, and that in mice the mortality was practically 100 per cent. On the other hand, his studies showed that rabbits, cats, dogs, and sheep seemed little affected.

He learned also that the eggs of the black widow spider represented a high degree of potency, and that two of them when crushed and emulsified in a drop of saline solution and injected intravenously or intraperitoneally proved sufficient to kill an adult white mouse. Upon being injected intravenously with a few drops of a saline emulsion of eggs a rabbit died within two minutes.

In 1935 Gray published a report. In it (and by letter to the authors) he told of two guinea pigs, each of which were given the full amount of toxin from both poison sacs of a mature female black widow spider. One of the animals experienced paralysis in its hind quarters, developed an intense diarrhea, exhibited labored respiration and heart action, and within one hour and fifty-six minutes after the injection died. The other registered only extreme illness.

Gray also reported that when 0.02 cc. of the venom was injected into a five-hundred-gram guinea pig, the suffering was intense, consisting of extreme excitement and pain. The animal then started to run madly around the cage, crying piteously, and within a very short time the hindquarters developed paralysis, which soon involved all the muscles, including those of respiration. The animal displayed a very profound watery diarrhea, and in this and similar cases death always ensued unless antivenom was administered.

In 1936 and 1938 D'Amour, Becker, and Van Riper studied the toxicity of the black widow spider's venom, as well as its chemistry, immunology and pathology. The total number of black widow spiders collected for such testings was about 6,500, and some five hundred rats were used. The toxicity of the spider's eggs, of the spiderlings, of the matured females and of the males was tested, and whereas the first three showed a progressive degree of potency, in the last instance the venom equivalent of twelve male spiders was injected into a rat with practically no resulting symptoms. On the other hand, in one series of experiments a venom equivalent of one-fourth of a female spider was injected into each of ten rats, resulting in a death rate of 50 per cent. Moreover, it was found that 0.064 mg. of spider venom killed 90 per cent of injected rats. In an experiment in which two prairie rattlesnakes were used, it was found that on a dry-weight basis the black widow spider's poison was fifteen times more potent.

Thus we note that significant results have almost invariably followed tests wherein black widow venom was used on animals. There were instances when certain animals were seemingly not affected, and in other experiments some of these animals, but not all, displayed symptoms. The probable causes for the discrepancies between the work of different investigators include variations in venom content of glands and amount of venom expelled, enzymatic destruction of venom, naturalization of venom by tissue juices, as well as differences in animals used, and nonspecific effect on the test subjects. The statement that the black widow venom is so much more toxic than the poison of snakes or other animal poisons may be true in terms of equal quantities of the different agents. The extremely small amount of the venom possessed by one spider at one time, however, makes this comparison misleading. Evidences of immunization were observed in a number of cases. Most revealing of all, however, was the fact that in a preponderance of cases severe symptoms developed, and death often followed.

10. Experiments with Latrodectus on Man

EXPERIMENTS conducted upon various animals have contributed much to the knowledge concerning black widow spider venom, but the only sure way to determine the effects of a poison on human beings is for the experimenters to test it upon themselves. In most cases of this kind, however, the experimenters employed species *other than* those belonging to the genus *Latrodectus*. Sanguinetti, Dufour, Erker, Heinzel, Walckenaer, Pickard-Cambridge, Blackwall, Duges, Harvy, Doleschall, Bertkau, Welsh, Fabre, McCook, and Simon allowed themselves to be bitten by spiders, and each stated that he was unable to detect any indication of resultant systemic poisoning. Further experiments conducted in the laboratory have justified these clinical testings.

Lucas and Bordas reported bites from *Latrodectus* as without any ill effects, but other clinical experiments show that such a bite results in severe pains, or—in instances where tests proved negative—that conditions of the experiment were at fault.

In 1915 Kellogg told of the experiments of a young graduate of medicine, E. H. Coleman, who had started a practice in the village of Los Altos, five miles from Stanford University at Palo Alto, California. Coleman, in his practice, was able to report a personal knowledge of two cases of black widow spider bites, both of which resulted in an immediate serious condition of the patients. He decided, moreover, to experiment upon himself. Accordingly he dissected the venom glands of a black widow spider, thereafter working the poison into a powdery mixture. He proceeded to take periodic doses during an interval of three days, and subsequently performed the experiment a second and third time. He reported that there were symptoms. Kellogg summed up the report by stating that he could "believe that it can be serious to some; for it has."

In 1922 Baerg experimented upon himself. In his instance the living spider was used. More than one test was made, and in the one that proved successful the spider was placed on the inner surface of the basal point of the third finger of the left hand; she bit as soon as placed and the fangs were allowed to remain inserted for about five seconds. Subsequently he was taken to the hospital where he was attended by Dr. E. F. Ellis. The clinical picture included difficult breathing; irregular and forced speech; pains or aches in the chest, hips, and muscles of the legs above the knee, and in the finger, hand, shoulder, and entire arm; delirium; fluctuation of body temperature; and pimples which in width measured from one and a half to two inches, and in length extended from the third finger on the outside of the hand to the elbow.

Summarizing, Baerg says that the most prominent feature in his case was the "sharp pain in the finger, or rather in the left hand." He asserts that "very nearly as unpleasant was the aching pain which was most violent in the thick muscles of the shoulders, chest and legs." In conclusion he states that the evidence in his experiment "shows that the bite of the Black Widow is likely to cause decidedly unpleasant, and under certain circumstances, dangerous results."

In 1923 Ewing experimented upon himself in a novel manner. Taking the entire contents of one poison sac of a matured female, he dissolved it in about 3 cc. of distilled water. He then washed the back of his left forearm with alcohol, after which he pricked it with a sterilized needle several times until it bled freely. A drop of the diluted aqueous solution of venom was subsequently placed over the wound and rubbed in with the point of the pipette. The resulting insignificant symptoms disappeared wholly in less than three hours.

During the afternoon of the next day he took 8 cu. mm. of the aqueous solution of the venom, and by means of a hypodermic syringe injected it into the left forearm. On the following morning he felt some pain, and at 6:39 P.M. reported that the skin was moist for a radius of about one inch "about the punctured pain." The area remained moist for several days, and there were further manifestations of pain.

Although the hypodermic injection consisted of much less than one per cent of the amount of venom necessary to completely fill one of the poison sacs, Ewing—with Baerg's experiment in mind—states that "the symptoms produced were almost identical with those that follow the bite of the spider."

In 1933 Blair played guinea pig to a black widow spider. At that time he was thirty-two years of age, in excellent health, was athletically inclined and weighed 168 pounds. Dr. Blair (in a letter to the authors) states that the bite was accidental in the first instance, but once started, the spider was permitted to complete it and data on the reaction were then recorded. The creature injected her fangs into the medial surface of the terminal phalanx of the little finger of the left hand.

Following the bite, the pain spread throughout the bitten finger, the hand, and finally the whole arm. There was some aching pain over the lateral surface of the left side of the chest. Following that came a dull, drowsy, lethargic and headachy feeling, together with aching pains in the muscles of the neck. The pulse became weak, and the respiration was deeper than normal. So serious did the symptoms become that about an hour and a quarter after the bite Blair turned over the taking of notes to assistants. Ten minutes later aching pains had affected the whole abdomen, and the legs had a flushed trembling feeling; it was decided to take him to the hospital, which was three miles distant. During the fifteen minutes en route the abdominal pains became more severe; aching pains manifested themselves in the region of the lower back; and the chest, besides registering pain, had a feeling of constriction. Speech became difficult and jerky, respirations rapid and labored, the abdomen rigid and boardlike, general appearance ashy colored with manifestations of cold sweat. The bitten finger became swollen, cyanotic, tender, and painful; the lips tense and contracted, causing the mouth to assume an oval shape. He complained of a slight dizziness and throbbing in the head, and there was profuse perspiration. In attendance was Dr. J. M. Forney, who first saw the patient two hours after having been bitten, when, as an initial treatment, he was reclining "in a tub of very warm water."

The report further tells of the patient complaining of pain in the back and legs as late as the second day, and there was tremor of the hands and a papular eruption on the inner surface of the bitten finger. The face was flushed and swollen, the tongue heavily furred, the breath foul, the abdomen tense. It was a full eight days after the beginning of the experiment before Blair could report that all signs and symptoms had disappeared. No better comment on the suffering he went through can be found than his answer to the question as to whether or not there is a development in man during convalescence of any degree of immunity to the venom of the black widow spider. He states that he was presented with the opportunity of deciding that point, but that he "lacked the courage" to submit himself to a possible repetition of the first experience.

These experiments furnish conclusive evidence that the black widow spider's bite may result in serious consequences to man. It is also interesting to note that in the instances where the black widow spider was induced to bite, the experimenters—because of the pain—very quickly had recourse to medical facilities and treatments. The dire effects from her bite, therefore, might have been even greater than those described if treatment had not been administered.

11. Diagnosis and Treatment of Black Widow Spider Bite

HISTORICAL records, medical reports, testimonials from spider-bite victims, and experiments by human guinea pigs all attest to the seriousness of *Latrodectus'* bite. Marked progress has been made in both diagnosis and treatment. Some spider victims escape without any ill effects, others suffer mildly, but not a few experience excruciating pains and, in some instances, death. Why this is so may now be explained.

Latrodectus, like other spiders, is equipped with a pair of fangs, but they differ from all others in that they are fed by unusually large poison glands. In addition to the poison contained in these sacs, the black widow spider's eggs are toxic, and, as first pointed out by Sachs and Kobert in regard to the European species of *Latrodectus*, her entire body is impregnated with a poison known as toxalbumen. "There is good evidence," according to Herms, Bailey, and McIvor, "that the poison sacs are not glandular in nature but function as absorptive organs which take up the poisonous constituents from the body fluid of the spider."

The fangs project from the head of the spider and can best be observed by means of the magnifying lens. They are technically described as *chelicerae*. Each is composed of a fleshy basal part and the claw, which latter section is commonly spoken of as "the fang." The fangs are hollow and the points curve toward each other. On the convex sides at their tip ends there are tiny openings, and these apertures emit the poison when the sharp points pierce the skin. They are so placed that they cannot be closed by pressure of the bite.

The second part of the venom apparatus is the poison glands that feed the fangs. They were observed over two hundred years ago by Anton van Leeuwenhoek (1632–1723), who sent descriptions of spider venom glands as seen under the microscope to the Royal Society in London. These glands are situated in the head-part of the spider, and are enclosed in a very fine, membrane-like sac, which as a rule may be extracted with the fangs. There is a poison pouch for each of the fangs, and in their relationship to the latter they are analogous to the bulb of an eye dropper. The venom sacs in *L. mactans* are longer than they are wide, and, as in all spiders, each curves outward and away from the sucking stomach. Nature has so ordained that the venom sacs will not press against a filled stomach and thus discharge their poison at an unpropitious moment.

These sacs are surrounded by a series of striated muscles, and the discharge of venom is occasioned by the compression of the sacs by these muscles, and not, as is commonly supposed, by the mechanical action of erecting the fangs. Most significant, too, is the fact that these muscles operate only at the volition of the spider; and this—the first factor which determines the seriousness of the bite of the creature—has far reaching implications. The black widow spider may strike one person without injecting any poison into the wound, and in another instance, only a small amount; in still another case, the maximum contained in a single sac, and in yet another a portion approximating the full content of her venom sacs. This obviously explains why certain victims of the black widow spider escape with a minimum of suffering while others experience agonizing pain.

It is also true that in some cases the spider may go through the motions of attacking one, and either will not be able to inject any poison, or the quantity that is injected will be comparatively small. There is a reason for this, and it is based upon scientific fact. Should the spider contact a human being shortly after she has expended her venom in subjugating an insect, the bite could not produce other than a mild effect. A victim of the black widow's bite can receive only the amount of poison that is present in the poison sacs at the time of the attack.

A third element which determines the seriousness of her bite is dependent upon the physical condition of the spider. A relative question concerns the size of the creature: whether or not she is fully matured, only approaching adulthood, or merely a spiderling; whether or not she is pregnant; and whether or not she has recently fed. Each of these anatomical features and environmental factors undoubtedly plays a part, however small, in determining the degree of suffering in a human victim. Since these are factors not readily determined, we must consider the black widow spider as a potential and ever-present danger.

A fourth determining factor concerns the temperament of *L. mactans*. The black widow spider does not make it a point to seek out mankind in order to inflict herself upon him. Indeed, insofar as *homo sapiens* is concerned she is a confirmed coward. When her web is disturbed by man she will—as we have learned—retreat into a far corner and, under certain circumstances, curl up her legs and "play dead." This inevitable action nevertheless offers little encouragement to mankind, since, in any case, a mentally well-balanced human being contacts the spider only by accident. Should one unconsciously or clumsily displace the black widow spider or annoy her by touch, she will bring her fangs into use simply as a means of self defense. This is a very special warning which should be given to children who have a tendency toward catching and playing with crawling things.

The fifth circumstance which has been mentioned as influencing the effects of the spider's bite concerns her foraging habit. In obtaining insects for her sustenance the black widow spider goes through a definite procedure. First, the prospective morsel is ensnared in her web. Then, as it struggles to free itself, the spider backs up to the creature, at the same time ejecting some strands of viscid silk, and by means of either one or both hind legs makes an effort to tie down the thrashing appendages. Should the victim continue its movements, she entangles it in some large, viscous droplets of material emitted from her spinnerets, and at the same moment brings her fangs into play. Because in attacking a human being the last operation only is performed, the probability suggests itself that in such case the spider finds herself confused at being balked in her regular routine. The surmise has been advanced that this momentary delay before the administration of the bite will provide one with an opportunity to remove the spider before the bite can be delivered. Actually, however, the creature bites a human being without warning; hence the hypothetical hesitancy is—for all practical purposes—inconsequential.

The sixth factor concerning the spider and its bite as related to mankind lies in the potentialities of the wound inflicted. The fangs or claws of the *chelicerae* of the black widow spider are approximately one fiftieth of an inch in length; hence, if inserted where the skin is thick and tough, they may not break through. Moreover, the depth to which they pierce even the thinnest epidermis may be determined only by her mood. Obviously if the spider is angered she will be prone to strike deeper than would otherwise be the case. Should the fangs penetrate to a sufficient depth, the poison may enter a blood or lymph vessel with damaging results; if otherwise, it may remain in the upper layers of the epithelium and do no harm. Further, the portion of the body upon which a person is bitten—with its relation to nerve centers—is a determining factor in the degree of seriousness of the bite.

The seventh and last factor is determined by the physical and mental condition of the victim. The toxin has a quantitative effect; therefore a given quantity would tend to be more dangerous to a child than to an adult. Alcoholics, syphilitics, and possibly persons affected with certain other diseases are likely to experience more serious consequences than would be the case with a healthy human being. In certain reported instances improper treatment has augmented the original ill conditions. On the other hand, delayed treatment, or none at all, has ofttimes resulted in greater suffering on the part of the patient. Certain individuals may be allergic to the poison, while others may have an uncommon form of resistance. Recorded cases indicate that the emotions of fear and excitement have added to the danger, and the recommendation has been made that the victim should remain calm. Presence of mind and common sense are always affirmative qualities.

And yet withal the most important factor in determining the seriousness of the bite is the first mentioned, i.e., the amount of poison the spider injects into the wound. The great potency of her venom is sometimes discounted by the fact that she on occasions rations out her poison, with the fortunate result that some victims escape with fairly light symptoms. This fact, however, should not induce bravado and false optimism in a victim to the extent of wishful thinking. The spider is no respecter of persons. The black widow spider has, as we have proved, a venom supply at her command sufficient—in its entirety—to cause intense suffering in any human being. Complications or physical weakness may bring death to the victim.

The question of correct diagnosis in black widow spider bite will now be considered. While it is quite true that the best way to determine whether one has been bitten by the black widow spider is to witness the creature in the act, it is also true that the spider is seldom caught in this compromising situation. Moreover, she leaves only minute fang pricks at the site of the bite, and these may be so tiny that they cannot be discerned with the naked eye. Waiving such conditions, the only certain way to decide whether or not a person has been bitten by the black widow spider is to compare his symptoms with those of former victims whose cases have been diagnosed as due to *Latrodectus.*

In general, the chain of symptoms is remarkably constant. When the spider inserts her fangs into the flesh of a human being, there is usually a mild, burning sensation, comparable to a sharp pin prick. This feeling endures for a few minutes only. The effects from the bite spread by continuity. In a typical case of a person who is bitten upon the palm of the hand, the pain will progress upward to the elbow, from thence to the shoulder area, and then down the trunk of the body toward the region of the kidneys, following which the abdomen becomes rigid. Or, as a further illustration, in a typical case of a patient being bitten on the buttock, penis, or scrotum, within from one-half to two hours a cramping sensation travels down the thigh, and a corresponding severe pain up the abdomen, which latter rigidity causes that portion of the body to become boardlike. There may be various other symptoms, including cold perspiration, an increase in blood pressure, a mild rise of body temperature, nausea and anorexia, vomiting, slight twitching or spasms of the muscles of the extremities, malaise, priapism, urinary retention, constipation, speech defect, insomnia, local edema, amnesia, difficult breathing, restlessness, cyanosis, depression, vertigo, chills, prostration or shock, paralysis, a macular skin eruption, jaundice, convulsion, tremors, muscle twitching, anxiety, and increase in the polymorphonuclear leukocytes and delirium.

In a careful analysis of the recorded symptoms, however, we find three significant phases. The first is the rapidity with which the poison is distributed throughout the body. In a typical case, the venom spreads with such dispatch that the characteristic pain appears within less than half an hour following the bite; it reaches its maximum intensity within an hour; and the general symptoms become evident within a few hours. The initial effects may be observed quite early, the interval between the bite and the first symptoms being sometimes a matter of only a few minutes. The venom of *L. mactans* possesses neurotoxic properties and particularly affects the nerves. Unlike rattlesnake venom, it does not affect the blood or blood vessels. The procedure used in snake bite—the application of the tourniquet—is an ineffective gesture in apprehending black widow poison.

The second important phase with regard to the symptom picture is the degree of pain experienced in various portions of the body. It is extremely severe and may be felt in the abdomen, legs, chest, arms—in fact throughout the body. Usually there are cramps and spasms in all of the larger muscles of the body. One report informs us that a victim of the black widow spider stated "he felt as if a current of electricity kept running through his arms and legs." Another patient has described the pain as not unlike huge tidal waves, with the whole body—as in a severe case of influenza—groaning with the so-called muscle and bone aches. So excruciating is the pain, according to numerous accounts, that the spider-bite victims roll and toss and moan in agony upon their beds of pain.

The third significant point regarding symptoms concerns the many genuine cases of black widow spider bite which have been wrongly diagnosed. Cases of arachnidism, or spider-bite poisoning, have been incorrectly diagnosed as acute pancreatitis, biliary or renal colic, tabetic crisis, food poisoning, tetanus, angina pectoris, enteritis, volvulus of stomach, coronary thrombosis, lobar pneumonia, diffuse peritonitis, an intussuception, and other ailments. In several instances black widow spider-bite victims have been examined by those who were at the time unfamiliar with the group of symptoms, and such cases were treated as patients afflicted with acute appendicitis. Under such erroneous diagnosis operations have sometimes been performed, and only long afterwards was the correct condition recognized and reported.

More frequently than any of these, however, black widow spider bite has been mistakenly diagnosed as ruptured gastric or duodenal ulcer. This is due to the fact that in repeated instances of black widow spider bite the abdominal wall became rigid and boardlike, which symptom is characteristic of ruptured ulcer. Because of the possibility of confusing the two, the line of demarcation should be outlined, and this has been worked out by Ginsburg. Spider bite gives a history of a bite, no history of ulcer symptoms, course of spread from bitten area to abdomen, mild or no collapse, temperature normal or slightly elevated, pulse slightly faster, cramp of extremities, X-ray negative for gas bubble, and the patient can sit up or move about. A ruptured ulcer gives no history of a bite, history of ulcer symptoms, knife-like pain at the point of rupture, collapse, temperature subnormal, no cramps of extremities, X-ray evidence of gas bubble in majority of cases, and the patient remains very quiet—does not want to be moved.

Finally, there is the question of treatment for the bite of the black widow spider. Divers treatments have been administered to those who have experienced the bite of this creature. Bogen states that more than seventy-five different remedies have been used, and our investigations increase the list to more than ninety. While a few of these have been helpful, and there are certain treatments which are definitely recommended, on the whole they have been fairly useless, and in some instances positively harmful. The remedies most often employed to counteract the poison were magnesium sulphate (Epsom salts), morphine, hot baths and fomentation, enemas, blood-letting, camphor and potassium permanganate, whiskey or brandy, aqua ammonia or spirits of ammonia, opium or tincture of opium, strychnine and atropine.

Among other remedies mentioned are arsenic, antimony, adrenalin, acetylsalicylic acid, aconitine, amidopyrine, amytal, aspirin, alkaline liquids, and amber; barbital, bromides, boneset, belladonna, and blood transfusion; castor calomel, cantharides, coal oil, cocain, calcium gluconate, caffeine, codeine, calcium lactate, cauterization with carbolic acid, and calcium chloride (intravenously); Dover's powders and Darby's fluid; edgewood, elaterium, Echniacea, and eucalyptol; glonoin, hoarhound, hyoscine, and hypochloride of lime; ipecac, indigo, iodine, and iodide and carbonate; luminal, and lavender; milk, magnesium phosphate, menthol, mercuric chloride, milk of magnesia, mercurochrome, magnesium citrate, mustard plasters, and nitro-glycerine; olive oil, phenol, plantain, potassium acetate, pantopon, and quinine; rue, soda, squirrel's ear, spirits of turpentine, salty grease, senna, sera, sodium chloride, sodium borate, and sinapisms; tansy, tartar emetic, tobacco poultice, volatile liniment and wizard oil.

Of these there are, including precautionary measures, several procedures that with varying degrees of helpfulness have been employed against the bite of the black widow spider. One is application of iodine to the site of the bite. L. *mactans* builds her web in such places as dusty corners, rubbish heaps and privies; potentially her fangs are laden with germs. There is a problem here as to treatment. While in some instances the site of the bite can be ascertained by a tiny reddish or whitish spot, in the majority of cases there is no clue other than a possible tingling sensation at the time of the injection. To prevent secondary infection, however, an effort should be made to determine the location of the insertion of the fangs, and iodine should be applied as a cauterizing agent.

Giving the victim hot baths is another procedure that has been used to combat the black widow's venom. As heretofore related, native spider-bite victims in southern Europe (during the late Middle Ages), and others in South Africa, indulged in a frenzied dance in order to induce heavy perspiration. Following this, they wrapped themselves in warm garments and rested or fell asleep on couches provided for the purpose. Here in the United States, Baerg, Blair, Walsh, and others discovered that hot baths are a beneficial therapeutic measure. In some patients a natural perspiration has been induced, which condition attests that nature herself has in certain instances used this means in an effort to rid the body of spider venom. Consequently it is usually suggested that the black widow spider victim be bathed in hot water, packed into bed beneath heavy woolen blankets, and surrounded with hot water bottles.

A comprehensive procedure used to combat black widow spider poison in a human victim includes several of the preceding measures. It has been employed with success at the General Hospital of Fresno County, California. In 1935 Frawley and Ginsburg first related the routine treatment used in that institution. In 1937 Ginsburg filed a report containing an additional therapeutic

The black widow spider as seen from above. Her shiny, black color, bulb-ous abdomen, and long, wiry legs make her easy to identify. Reports testify to her presence in each of the forty-eight states. Scientifically known as Latrodectus mactans, she has gone under a variety of common names, most of which are based upon some characteristic of hers. Certain Indians of California called her Po-ko-moo. Throughout the United States she has been called the hourglass spider, the southern spider, the deadly spider, the T-spider, the poison lady, the shoe-button spider, the poison spider, and the black spider. With the turn of the century, however, the name, black widow, came into general use.—Photo by Wayne Book.

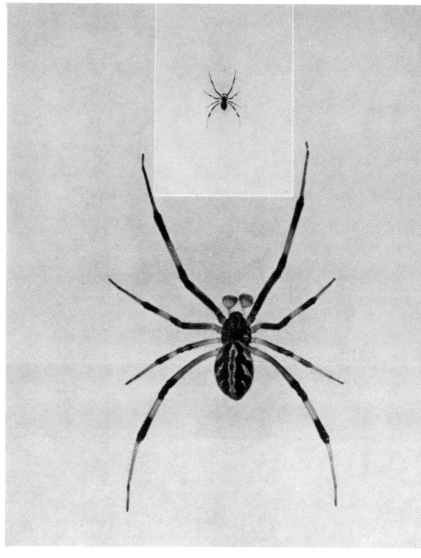

Mature male black widow spider. (Inset shows natural size.) Observe bulb endings of the leg-like feelers (pedipalpi), a characteristic of all male spiders. The male of this species is from one-third to one-half the size of the female. Very likely he will have four vertical stripes running along the sides of his abdomen, a dark band down the middle of the front part of his body, and another, but of different design, along the midsection of his back. Like his spouse, he may have the hourglass figure beneath the abdomen, but it tends to be dull and hardly recognizable. His venom is incapable of causing injury to a human being. Contrary to popular belief, the female eats the male black widow only when in direst hunger.—Photo by W. B. Herms.

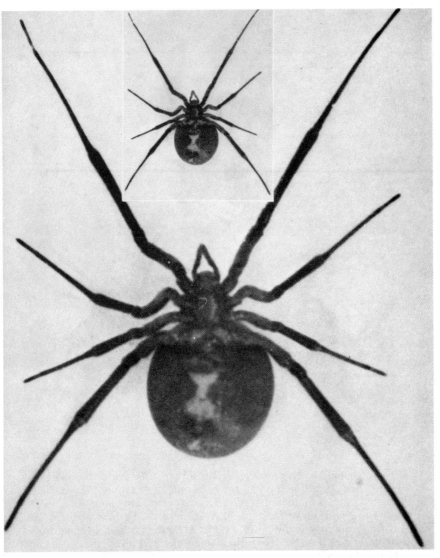

The black widow spider in an up-side down position. (Insert shows natural size.) Observe the hourglass design underneath the abdomen, which may be colored yellow, orange, or red. There are three varieties of this species, each tending to have its zone of habitation—the eastern and central states, the southwestern states, and all states west of the Rocky Mountains. One may have a red spot on the back above the spinnerets, or that color may extend as a band along the dorsal part; another may have a red streak just above the spinnerets and also a small white mark on the anterior end. The one referred to most in recent literature, however, is wholly black except for the red or orange or yellowish hourglass design. —Photo by Wayne Book.

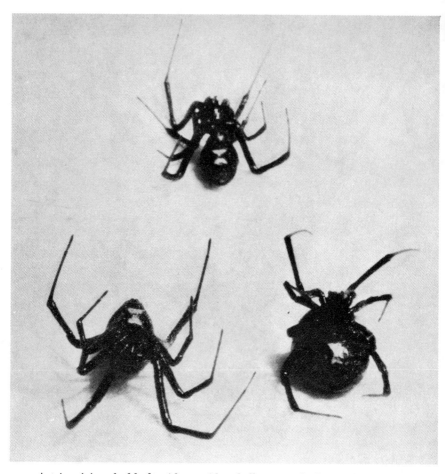

A trio of female black widow spiders belly upwards. Note the hourglass designs. The one at the top is at the beginning of gestation, the lower left hand specimen is in an advanced stage, and the one to the right is about ready for deposition of her eggs. She usually deposits them at night. At such time she may be found in an up-side down position, hanging from a strand of web near the rim of the framework of an inverted webbed cup attached to her nest. She begins a swaying motion, and at the proper pitch the butter-colored, ball-like eggs are forced out into the receptacle. When the last ones have been expelled, she turns her spinnerets until they are close to the eggs and emits a viscid silk. With her rear legs she works it around and over until the egg sac has been completely enclosed. It is watertight and of sufficient toughness to insolate the contents from practically all insect predators. The deposition of the eggs and the construction of the cocoon consume at least an hour, and may require as much as three hours.—Photo by Newton Berlin.

ABOVE: *The black widow spider hovering over her egg sacs. These usually are within her web, where she—belly upwards—may be found guarding them. When engaged upon a foray of destruction against the black widow spider, it is necessary to destroy the egg sacs as well as the spider.*—Photos by Newton Berlin.

BELOW: *Illustrating the alacrity with which the black widow spider makes her getaway. In the foreground are her egg sacs. Because of her cowardly hit-and-run tactics, she is seldom seen until the victim has received the stroke—and not always then.*

Black widow spider's web. Note that it is coarse and irregular with little design other than a zig-zag, criss-cross network. In a spiderling's nest, the strands of silk are few and short of length; but with passing of time— should her location afford space—the webbed nest may be enlarged to a three-foot diameter. Selecting a position often near the apex of the web, she will spin an extra number of strands to form a kind of pocket which constitutes her inner castle. The periodic ravages of the elements and of insect destroyers make it necessary to repair the original work from time to time. On occasion, because of some annoyance, she may desert her abode and move to another site, there to construct a similar nest.—Photo by W. B. Herms.

She builds her nest in the dark corners of basements, garages, and attics, and in hundreds of other locations convenient for attaching a web. This one was found underneath a frame house. This species has been discovered under the seats of privies, behind shutters, in rain spouts, within bundles of old letters, beneath shelves, in book stacks, shoe boxes, pump houses, in cellars, tool sheds, piles of automobile casings, under board walks, in man-holes, metal waste containers, and smoke houses, on rafters, in unused flower pots and meter boxes, under steps, and in tile roofs. Reports further tell of her presence in unusual places—in the sleeve of a work shirt, under a rocking chair, in a shoe, and in the framework of a scarecrow.—Photo by Keith Boyd.

A spider with three egg sacs scattered in her coarse, criss-cross web. The interval between the successive cocoons varies from about one week to four months. Each sac contains from 25 to 1000 eggs. During her life span of a little more than a year, she may spin and fill a total of nine egg sacs. The length of time the embryonic young remain within the egg sac varies from about four days in summer to about one month in cold weather. When the moment arrives for their emergence, they make one or more holes in the fabric and then, singly, squeeze through and out into the web of their parent, who is within watchful distance. In the tip-of-the-thumb size world which has been theirs, they leave behind their discarded skins.—Photo by Wayne Book.

Here up above and to the right of the spider is a bee which she has swathed with silk. The white ball is her egg sac. This spider has a come-what-may menu and often catches unusual creatures in her web. Life records of one specimen totaled 240 domestic flies, 3 grasshoppers, and 2 garden spiders; another 255 domestic flies, 12 sowbugs, and 3 grasshoppers; a third, 197 domestic flies, 7 sowbugs, and a small centipede; a fourth, 163 domestic flies, 2 nocturnal moths, one grasshopper, and one Jerusalem cricket; and a fifth, 173 domestic flies, 21 vinegar flies, and 3 grasshoppers. These observations are from a single locality. Feeding records in other districts would differ in their insect prey.—Photo by Wayne Book.

A specimen housed in a glass jar for observation purposes. The lid to the container should be screwed tight but perforated to provide air. Note her web attached to the two sticks and the fly that was cast in as food. This spider, both in captivity and in a wild state, shows evidence of great tidiness. After she has quelled an insect, she may permit the morsel to remain trussed up at the location of the kill; or it may be conveyed to the pocket of her nest, where at her leisure she devours it. When once the life juices have been removed, she cuts all points of attachment between the web and the body-shell, permitting the latter to fall free amid the husks of previous victims.—Photo by Wayne Book.

ABOVE: Numerous newspaper accounts have related incidents wherein persons staged battles between black widow spiders and scorpions, tarantulas, solpugids and any one of a dozen or more similar creatures.

BELOW: The black widow spider assumes the death posture—legs curled up—when roughly disturbed. When she feels safe she unfolds her legs and resumes normal activity. She may display similar subterfuge when efforts are made to drown her with bland oil or water. Washed down from her perch by the deluge, she simply curls up and remains quiescent until the inconvenience is over. She owns characteristics of hardiness which in their combination far exceed those of many other creatures of Insecta and Arachnida.—Photo by Newton Berlin.

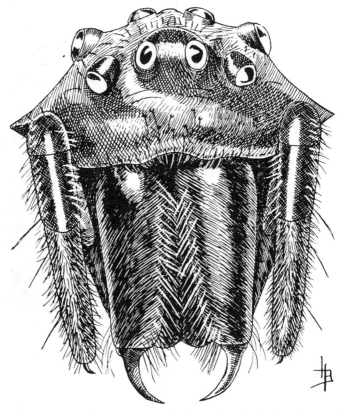

Drawing showing the enlarged head of the female black widow spider (front view). Note her eight eyes and the claws or fangs (chelicerae) which bend in toward each other. They are approximately one-fiftieth of an inch in length, hollow, and near their tip is a tiny opening which is an outlet for the poison that, when introduced into man, has resulted in great suffering and, under certain conditions, death. The poison glands that feed the fangs are situated in the head-part of the spider. The poison sacs are surrounded by striated muscles which operate at the will of the spider. Hence she may strike one person without injecting any poison into the wound, whereas another may receive the maximum contents. This fact largely explains the discrepancies in black widow spider bite reports.—Photo by U. S. Department of Agriculture.

measure and later, in communication with the authors, furnished additional data. At the institution noted above the routine treatment consists of the following procedure:

1. The patient is immediately put to bed and iodine is applied to the site of the bite. Absolute bed-rest for twenty-four hours is imperative.

2. A soap-suds enema is administered, and fluids, non-alcoholic, are given freely via the mouth.

3. Morphine sulphate, grain one-quarter, is administered hypodermically to control the pain, and sodium amytal, grains iii, to insure rest.

4. Magnesium sulphate, a 20 cubic centimeter ampoule of 10 per cent solution, is given intravenously, to be repeated as required to overcome hypertension and the spasticity of the muscles.

5. Glucose, 10 per cent, is administered intraveneously if the patient's condition demands it.

The regimen described by Ginsburg will give good results in most cases, magnesium sulphate having been so used in Los Angeles long before (and later by De Asis and others), but the calcium treatment introduced by Stewart and Gilbert seems to be a definite improvement, and may render the administration of morphine, amytal, etc., unnecessary. Also in some cases a spinal puncture may be valuable, especially in instances of marked increase in blood pressure with threatening cerebral symptoms.

Another procedure practiced to counteract the poison of the black widow spider is the use of serums. The development of an effective antivenin was long the hope of those physiological chemists who have done pioneer work in the study of the venom of *Latrodectus*. Beginning in the latter part of the nineteenth century, and on through the years, various persons have worked on, or reported concerning, spider-poison serum. These scientists variously represented Europe, South America, and the United States, and they include Sczerbina, Rossikov, Konstansoff, Brazil, Vellard, Moore, Amaral, Troise, Gray, Berman, Smith, Becker, Van Riper, Bogen, Hall, and D'Amour.

Studies by Bogen, Hall, and D'Amour showed the practicability of the development of animal sera from rats, guinea pigs, rabbits, and larger animals. During the middle 1930's the American public at large began to take an interest in *L. mactans* and several of the pharmaceutical houses marketed black widow spider antivenin. Mulford Biological Laboratories of Sharp and Dohme have developed a dehydrated serum in lyophilized form (spider antivenin). Several favorable reports have been received following its use. The most noteworthy experiments along this line, however, were conducted at the Los Angeles County General Hospital. It was in July of 1925 that the use of human convalescent serum in the treatment of arachnidism was first tried at the Los Angeles County Hospital, the results therefrom being reported by Bogen in 1926. It consisted "in the separation of the serum from the whole blood taken from patients who had recovered from a characteristic spider-bite poisoning from two weeks to twelve months previously. Varying doses, usually about ten to twenty cc., were given subcutaneously, or intramuscularly."

Although Bogen declares that the theoretical soundness and occasional value of the serum are unquestioned, he nevertheless states that the results are not so striking as to make it the most valuable treatment. He recommends the calcium treatment for arachnidism, which was developed by Stewart and Gilbert at the Los Angeles County General Hospital. This consists of the intravenous injection of 10 cc. of 10 per cent calcium chloride or gluconate. "So effective is it in overcoming the symptoms of spider bite poisoning," states Bogen, "that the use of serum is now not often indicated. . . ."

It may be true—as stated by several investigators—that in a typical case in which the patient is robust "the entire process from effects of the bite will subside in a short while even without any treatment being rendered." So many are the factors involved in black widow spider bite, however, that whatever the physical condition of the patient, it is most unwise to underestimate its possible effect. The most important consideration of all, as before stated, involves the quantity of poison received by the victim. And since there is no practical test to determine the amount of venom so introduced in any given case, it behooves one who has been bitten to call upon a physician who is familiar with arachnidism treatment.

12. The Black Widow Spider
Before the Public

~~~~~~

MUCH of the foregoing has been concerned with the scientific aspects of spider bite. A phase to be considered deals with the interest the general public has taken in the black widow spider. Since 1934, the press has contained many references to this creature. This does not mean, however, that press notices on the black widow spider were lacking in previous years. One investigator has on file a scrap book full of clippings beginning before 1926. There have been periodic outbursts of interest in spider bite. In the year 1934, there was an especially notable wave of popular interest in the black widow spider, and it may be entertaining to review the nature of publicity given the creature during this period.

The daily press carried on the discussion of the black widow spider from various angles. Much interest was displayed by lay people concerning the locations in which the black widow spider constructs her web. One account concerned a nest of spiders that was found on the bottom of a chair. Another explained that certain vineyardists and tomato croppers were compelled to let their fruit rot because the vines were said to be infested with black widow spiders. This latter report was costly to the grower, as the pickers read the article and refused to work. One item mentioned the claim-jumping, by a black widow spider, of a police call box. Another recounted that a black widow spider had built her nest in a corner of the front seat of an automobile which was in storage. When the owner of the machine, a youth of high school age, decided to put the car into operation he was astounded to discover the creature ensconced therein with a brood of newly hatched young. Thus the press accounts have from time to time itemized the proved habitats of the black widow spider, these ranging from picture frames to the drawers of wardrobe chests.

In addition, there have been numerous newspaper accounts telling of instances wherein persons staged battles between black widow spiders and scorpions, tarantulas, small species of snakes, cockroaches, centipedes, or any one of a dozen or more similar creatures. The participants were dubbed with titles befitting fighters, and the progress of the encounters was posted in the press from day to day. At the height of interest several of these combats involving such creatures were conducted simultaneously in various sections of the country. Field days were enjoyed by news correspondents in comparing one match with another. Over night, so it appeared, the sponsors of such frays received nation-wide mention, and so frantic became the competition that within the twenty-four hours following, their names were replaced by those of others who had conceived of new challengers to the spider, as the tomato worm, harvestman, squash bug, ground beetle, and silver-fish. Infrequently the exhibitions were permitted to run their course, but usually humane society or city officials interfered and stopped them. The bouts were held in private homes and in garages, pool rooms, and men's club houses; but the vast majority took place—for advertising purposes and to lure potential customers—in show windows of shops which merchandised articles ranging upward or downward from dog food to a newly-patented can opener. At times the black widow spider was confronted by a creature which she found it easy to vanquish, and at other times the strategic position acquired by either antagonist determined the outcome of the battle. She numbered among her victims creatures many times her weight in which the advantage, it would seem, was on the side of her opponent. In every instance, the course of the battle was followed with equal interest by those who witnessed it and the multitudes who read the day-by-day accounts in the newspapers. Some persons asserted that the encounters were bestial, and that the sponsors were only exhibiting their own hitherto repressed and innate barbaric tendencies. Others declared that the bouts were educational in that they called attention to the prolific increase of mankind's enemy in the world of nature.

Since 1934 there have been newspaper accounts that related incidents concerning the black widow spider which, by their unique nature, placed her in a category apart from all other creatures. One item concerned a newspaper reporter who undertook an experiment with a black widow spider in a mortuary. This story earned nationwide importance over a period of several days. In the presence of a physician, two photographers, an ambulance driver, a newspaperman, and several witnesses (and the undertaker), he "teased, coaxed and squeezed the black widow, but all to no avail." The spider scampered about his hand, "crawling in and out of his fingers spinning a web." The reporter, so the dispatches said, "denied that he was nervous, but his hand shook as the spider crawled about." After half an hour of this, with the spider steadfastly refusing to bite, the reporter gave up the experiment and said that he would try to get a more "aggressive" specimen and repeat the test the following week. For some reason the second experiment was never undertaken.

Worth noting is the story concerning a thirty-two-year-old experimenter who was bent on devising a preparation which would "kill every known type of insect," and also black widow spiders. He tried his formula on moths, ants, black beetles, boll weevils, bed bugs, termites, and cheese mites, and the resulting destruction proved satisfactory (to himself) in each instance. To apply the test to the black widow spider, however, he decided to procure a large supply of this species of spiders and accordingly got in touch with a spider dealer. During the course of his experiments the amateur scientist received several shipments, the last of which contained fifty black widow spiders. Obtaining the creatures from the express office, he placed the containers housing them in his car, which subsequently was left parked in a city street. He later returned to the spot and found that his car, spider shipment and all had been stolen. To an inquiring reporter he stated—not in anger—his fears for the safety of the thief. For some reason the newspapers dropped the "scientist," who was never heard of again.

Workers who were grading a new parade ground at a certain naval station encountered a gigantic black widow spider breeding nest, the adult females and spiderlings comprising many thousands of individuals. The infested area covered the two-acre parade ground, and also the surrounding tract of land which embraced a much larger acreage. It was decided to destroy the dangerous colony. Seventy or more men participated, a large proportion of whom were engaged in turning over every stone in the vicinity, opening wider every crevice in the earth, and lifting every piece of brush. Following this advance guard were others operating blow torches, which were similar in construction to those of the hogburner type used in foundries. With fifteen feet of hose, they threw out a flame six inches in diameter at the nozzle, which at thirty inches became a twenty-four inch flame striking the earth under a thirty pound pressure. Inch by inch these operators went over the ground, searing every possible hiding place of the black widow spiders.

Much attention was also given to the black widow spider by columnists and comic-strip writers. Some of the medical columns described the black widow and mentioned a few of the most striking symptoms, admonishing those readers unfortunate enough to run afoul of the spider to get in touch with their family physician at once. Other commenting columnists represented a variety of types from news commentators to gag writers. Many exuded a naïve philosophy regarding the black widow spider and her place in the realm of nature; others conveyed factual data pertaining to the creature; and still others—with humor—made capital of the attempts by certain organizations to halt the highly publicized fights in which the black widow spider was one of the combatants.

Cartoonists of the large dailies drew upon the news value of the black widow spider in a multiplicity of ways. Her criss-cross, coarsely woven web proved to be a convenient contrivance in conveying ideas. Also her color of glossy black, together with her eight wiry legs, afforded unlimited opportunities for the artist to submit a thought conveying horror. But the spider's yellow, orange, or red hourglass design captured the highest degrees of pictorial interest, especially when used as a symbol of death. Indeed, the whole assembly of physical characteristics made a most fitting vehicle by which to deliver the artist's message.

The comic-strip writers utilized the black widow spider theme as a fantastic novelty. In one instance De Beck, as the plot of his strip, had the "sargent" and his men on the trail of a notorious woman crook, who, with her cohort, had obtained "the ransom notes" and was bent upon a quick getaway via plane. The only clues the law enforcement officers had to work with were one of the woman's slippers and her alias of the "Black Widow Spider." In another instance Segar placed his chief character in the role of adviser to his youthful readers. The "adviser" described the spider as a small, black creature with a red mark on her underside shaped like an old-fashioned hourglass. He advised his readers not "to play around" in garages or cellars where there is rubbish or lumber, or in attics or wood shed, "for these are some of the places where the black widow has her habitat." This character of the comics gave much wholesome counsel, advising his readers that the poison from the black widow spider is "more potent than that of a rattlesnake," and that "if a person is bitten he should see a doctor immediately."

Other means than the newspaper of broadcasting information concerning the black widow spider included the radio, the magazines, and motion pictures. Frequently the radio newscaster with a sectional audience mentioned local cases of spider bite. He detailed the agonizing pains experienced by the victims and the measures which had been taken in an effort to stave off more serious consequences. Less frequently, the comments regarding the creature were heard from coast to coast.

Magazine articles by the score treated the subject of the black widow spider. Such accounts appeared in manifold types of popular periodicals, including garden, travel, scientific, outdoor, farm, and motion picture magazines. Usually the articles were written by scientists whose field had been other than the arachnological, or by physicians who had not specialized in medical entomology. At other times the contributions were signed by lay feature writers, whose personal observations and investigations regarding the subject were nil. Some of the articles published contained fairly accurate information, while others were erroneous, and some even ludicrous. As a rule, however, they were instrumental in arousing a healthful interest on the part of the public in the widespread danger caused by the increase in this species of *Latrodectus*.

The black widow spider was used in literary treatments in a number of ways. The comic-strip artist was not alone in fastening upon his female suspect the title of the "Black Widow Spider." The newspapers of a leading metropolis used the first two words of this name, inclosed by quotation marks, in reference to a female character who was then under investigation. A semi-fiction detective magazine of the pulp variety had for its cover a replica of a black widow spider dangling from its web above a horror-stricken woman. The lead story, "The Black Widow," dealt not with a spider but with a European woman criminal who over a span of years murdered a number of persons in order to collect their insurance. Differing from this, one writer in a simile declared that the "deadliest Communists are like the black widow spider; they conceal their *red* underneath." (Italics his.)

The black widow spider was also used as a subject for motion pictures. This was possibly stimulated in part by the interest exhibited by the actors, several of whom later became tyro arachnologists voicing opinions as to the poisonous propensities of this spider. The interest manifested by the public at large resulted in the production of a film in which the plot revolved around the black widow spider. In the sequence there were a number of mysterious murders, and finally the death weapon was discovered upon the body of a would-be victim—in form of a capsule containing a black widow spider. The clever plot entailed the melting of the capsule and the liberation of the creature, which thereupon bit her host.

The black widow spider was thrust before the public in many other ways. The practical joker seized upon it with sinister glee. Imitations of the spider were sold in fun shops. Once such a toy had been purchased, the object was to stealthily place it upon some portion of a friend's clothing and then shout "Black Widow!" In one community a bank placed a glass jar containing a black widow spider and her brood in its window display; in another part of the country a drug store followed the same idea and more than five thousand persons viewed it. School teachers brought specimens—safely housed in fruit jars—to class rooms; and the pupils were thus taught methods of positive identification.

The safety engineer for a mammoth bridge under construction issued a dodger entitled "The Black Widow."

He described the appearance of the creature, explained the construction of her egg sac, and depicted her webbing as "*heavy and strong; irregular in shape with no symmetrical design.*" He stated that she may be found in dark, dry corners and crevices, as under edges of storage tanks, and in warehouses, sheds, garages, and "draw-off boxes." He advised workmen to keep clean any likely abodes for the spider, destroy web and eggs, and crush all black widow spiders that were found. He gave the typical symptom picture resulting from its bite and offered suggestions as to treatment.

Attempts at suicide or at murder, using the black widow spider as the lethal weapon, have been featured in the newspapers. We unwittingly had a part in the publicity attending a suicide which took place in 1935. On June 3, news dispatches and radio broadcasts stated that a young man by the name of Stephen Liarsky, of Worcester, Massachusetts, had died from the self-induced bite of a black widow spider. The creature supposedly responsible for this fantastic suicide was found in a tiny cardboard box on a table near the young man's unconscious body. The victim had obtained this spider from us, he (not aware of the prevalence of *Latrodectus* in New England) having requested that a California specimen be sent to him for observation purposes. After the first announcement regarding the suicide, however, a pronouncement by the physicians conducting the post-mortem inquiry discounted the spider angle, but upheld the suicide as one consummated through a heavy overdose of narcotics. The clues for this last diagnosis were the symptom picture and the finding in the suicide's room of an empty bottle which had once held powerful sleeping potions.

Accounts of murder attempts by means of spider bite may be found in the literature of by-gone years as well as in recent times. History relates that in the examination into the murder of Sir Thomas Overbury, one of the witnesses stated that "the countess wished him to get the strongest poison that he could. . . . He accordingly brought seven great spiders." In the murder case of James, a master barber who resided in southern California, the newspapers told of his forcing his wife to place her foot into a box containing rattlesnakes, "and of submitting her to black widow spiders." Homicide did not result therefrom, however, and murder was ultimately carried out by drowning in a bath tub.

Finally, the question of payment of insurance claims for spider bite has been given notice in the newspapers within recent times, and this phase of popular attention has aroused the interest of members of the legal profession. One newspaper account related that the wife of .a black widow spider victim brought suit in an effort to compel a company to pay double indemnity on insurance policies held by the deceased. The courts were asked to define death from the bite of a black widow spider as "violent and accidental." That claims are actually being honored is proved by the fact that one insurance company alone lists four payments for "spider bite" in a single report. One of these cases concerned a male who was paid three claims for spider bite, the amount totaling $58.31. Another pertained to a male, a welder by trade, who received only $2.80 for his claim. The third, a male, was paid five claims (injured arm varicocele, pneumonia, doctor bill, and spider bite), and the payments to him totalled $198.97. The fourth, a male and a rancher by occupation, was given $28.33 for one claim—spider bite. These citations become all the more significant when one realizes that insurance companies make payments only after a thorough investigation and with a firm conclusion that the claim is bona fide.

While newspaper and other forms of publicity served to arouse the public interest and thereby create talk concerning the creature, the savants were conducting investigations as to the origin of this interest. One reason for the public's interest is the fact that progressively increasing opportunities are being afforded for persons to come in contact with the creature. Before the country had become extensively settled the black widow spider inhabited only the wilds. Nature's balance, including birds and wasps, kept her numbers regulated; the rains periodically soaked her egg sacs and thus each season destroyed an effective proportion of the young. Climaxing these developments, the white man came upon the scene, ploughing under the fields and hewing down the woods. The black widow spider, thus divested of her natural habitat, moved into the wood piles, the barns, and human habitations. With rural life tending to give way to urban life, and with the increase of population, the spider menace becomes increasingly more pronounced.

Another reason why the black widow spider has, of late years, received such extensive notice is that, as a result of such contributions as Bogen's, the medical profession is more prone to recognize cases of black widow spider bite. In earlier instances the pain induced by the bite of the creature was often attributed to some other disease. Even those doctors who suspected that a tiny spider might possibly be the instrument of so much agony hesitated, in view of the skepticism of their fellows, in making such diagnosis. But with the recent publication in medical journals of authoritative case histories and with many physicians now in possession of the symptom picture, there has been reported an increasing number of instances of arachnidism.

The third reason for the late nation-wide recognition of the black widow spider is directly connected with the reported multiplication of the species. There are two conclusions regarding this. One is the belief that because of the mild winter which prevailed through the country in 1933–34, myriads of the spiders were able to survive and thus bring forth phenomenal families. That year also ushered in a big drought, the heat thus generated enabling a greater percentage of the eggs to hatch and the young to develop to maturity. Others doubt the purported increase in, or greater prevalence of, spiders during the stated period. They admit that the seasonal fluctuations are marked, but they point out the fact that in the decade or more prior to 1934 numerous black widow spiders were also noted. They declared that very early accounts mention an abundance, and state further that when change of habitat has occurred it was with decrease rather than increase in the species, on account of the abolition of such facilities as the old fashioned privy. They conclude that while fluctuations do occur according to weather conditions, change in frequency of natural enemies, and other factors, publicity and consequent greater attention and recognition seem to have resulted in an imaginary increase.

13. Latrodectus Mactans in the Araneid Scheme

‹‹

UP TO this point we have discussed the black widow spider's history, its relation to mankind, the effects of its venom upon a human being, various treatments for the bite, and the fact that it represents the only dangerous species in the United States. There remain three phases concerning the spider yet to be considered. One pertains to its proper classification and another to its life habits. The third is in the nature of a problem. This problem in many respects equals, and in others surpasses, the task that medical men have faced through the years in establishing a symptom picture and working out a treatment for the creature's bite. It concerns, briefly, methods devised and under advisement to bring the spider under control and to lessen its numbers.

The proper classification of the black widow begins with a discussion of the line of demarcation between spiders and insects. Some persons have, although rarely, spoken of the black widow spider as an animal, and very often the layman has referred to it as an insect. This last is not strange, as in past years the scientists have themselves included spiders among the *Insecta*. It is erroneous, however, to say that a spider is an insect, and in explanation we shall indicate the dissimilarity between the two.

It is necessary to mention the kinship between the spider and insect. Both belong to the phylum *Arthropoda*, which in addition to the spiders and insects includes the crabs, the lobsters, the millipedes, and the scorpions. This is the largest of the phyla of the animal kingdom and embraces many more species than all others combined. All of the *Arthropoda* possess articulated bodies and jointed legs, are diminutive as compared with some other forms of life, and in contrast with those creatures that belong to the phylum *Vertebrata*, which own a framework of true bones, they have for their skeleton only the external skin.

Despite these similarities, there are striking differences between the spider and insect. The spider has eight legs, a matured insect only six. The first has two body sections —the cephalothorax (in which the head and thorax are combined) and the abdomen; the second, three—the head, the thorax, and the abdomen. The spider is without true antennae and instead has leg-like feelers designed as pedipalpi, or the palpi; and the insect is equipped with genuine insect wireless apparatus. The former is wingless; in a majority of the species the latter, at certain stages, owns flying appendages. The spider, a carnivorous creature, injures no food plants; many of the herbivorous insects yearly destroy vast acreages of agricultural crops.

And there are still other differences. The spider is provided with smooth, simple eyes, some of which, in order to afford sight in more than one plane, are situated in certain positions on the upper part of the front portion of her body. The insect is furnished with compound eyes divided into innumerable facets which afford greater power of vision. Although both spiders and insects breathe through air tubes, or tracheae, located at certain points on their bodies, the former possess book lungs. These appendages are air sacs which may be found on the under side of the abdomen near the base or fore part, and appear like two semi-lunar patches of a color lighter than that which surrounds them. These peculiar organs are made up of leaf-like folds, which fact accounts for the name "book lungs." The spider further differs from the insect in that it has no true jaws, the openings of the reproductive organs are near the front of the abdomen, and there is not a conspicuous metamorphosis.

The spider is a spinner of silk-like web, and the various species fashion a galaxy of patterns that are known throughout the world. Even those females which depend the least on constructing snares to catch prey must use web to enclose their clusters of eggs. Insects in some instances manufacture silk, but it comes from an attachment next to the mouth and not, as is the case with spiders, from the finger-like protuberances at the rear of the abdomen, called spinnerets. Web in most instances is the material with which spiders build their homes, fashion the cradles for their young, and construct the traps to capture food.

But really to understand the characteristics of a spider, and, in particular, the black widow, it is necessary to study the creature's external and internal anatomy. The naked eye at first glance discerns a creature with long, black, wiry legs which, when stretched to the full, give it a leg spread of as much as two inches. The black widow, like all spiders, is divided into two parts—the cephalothorax and the abdomen. The fore section is comparatively tiny, while the latter—especially when with eggs—rounds up prominently, often measuring as much as ⅜ by ½ inch. The spider appears to be bald and in color is shiny black, with a red, orange, or yellow hourglass insignia on the underside of its abdomen. These are the features visible to the naked eye.

By the use of the hand lens and with careful scrutiny, additional features will come into the view of an observer. There are, for instance, those which are associated with the fore part of the body, or cephalothorax. The top portion of this section of the spider is composed of a hard shield known as the carapace. The eyes, eight in number, are situated upon the fore end of the shield. They are pearly white, a fact indicating nocturnal optical powers. Projecting from the front part of her body are the fangs and leg-like feelers, known as the pedipalpi, between which is the mouth cavity. The mouth being fitted only for the reception of liquid foods, the spider alternately sucks and presses its victim which, after being emptied of its juices, is thrown aside. The eight legs are attached to the under side of the cephalothorax, and each is divided into seven segments which, beginning with the one next to the body, bear the names of coxa, trochanter, femur, patella, tibia, metatarsus and tarsus. The last segment of the fourth pair of legs of the black widow spider has attached a comb that consists of a row of strong curved and toothed hairs with which the creature flings viscid silk over the insect-prey entangled in her web.

Secondly, lens observations reveal several interesting characteristics regarding the rear part of the spider's body —the abdomen. While to the naked eye it looks smooth and glossy, there appear under magnification evidences of a coating of almost infinitesimal hairs. On the under side may be seen the paler-colored patches, the lung books, and between them the opening of the reproductive organs. The spinning organs, or spinnerets, which in the black widow number six, are to be seen protruding from the rear, and just above them is the anus. All of the above-named characteristics—those pertaining to the cephalothorax and the abdomen—compose the essential visible external features of the black widow spider.

Bringing into play forceps and needles, scissors and scalpels, a dissection of the black widow spider may be accomplished and her internal anatomy examined. When this is done, the pedicle, a slender stalk connecting the cephalothorax and abdomen (which in most spiders is hidden by an overhanging portion of this latter section), will be revealed. Even in large spiders its diameter is small, but despite this it encloses an artery, the nerve cord, and a part of the gut. Features may be found in the cephalothorax of the spider which include the poison glands, brain and the fore-intestines, the last-mentioned consisting of the pharynx, the oesophagus, and the sucking stomach. The mid and hind intestine, the internal reproductive organs, the silk glands, and the heart, as well as less important parts, are all enclosed in the spider's abdomen.

In order to comprehend the make-up of the black widow spider more fully, however, it is imperative for one to know the quality and function of her outer covering—the skin or cuticula—as well as facts concerning the creature's growth. The skin is composed of hard chitin, a substance analogous to that which makes up the human finger-nails, and is indestructible to the degree that it is insoluble in most of the strong acids. Muscles are attached, and the hard substance serves the dual purpose of bones and armor. By intervals the spider acquires a new skin, and it, being flexible, permits the internal parts to develop and expand. In time—as a result of exposure to the air— the skin becomes hard and inelastic, and the spider approaches a condition whereby there is little room remaining for a further increase in size. At this point, in order that the creature may continue to grow and reach maturity, the old skin must be discarded to make way for the new. This is known as the process of moulting.

Moulting proceeds in the following manner. Prior to the performance, a new, elastic skin has been formed beneath the old, through which fluid glands loosen the unwanted cuticula. The aged skin splits and is shed in a specific fashion. First, the cuticula of the front part of the spider, and then that of the abdomen, shears off. Next, the creature works its eight legs out of their well-aged boots, and so neatly and in whole is the skin discarded that a first glance frequently mistakes the empty shell for the living spider. The time required for moulting depends upon first, the species of spider, and second, the age of the creature, since a youngling moults more speedily than does a specimen approaching adulthood. In a typical case of a nearly grown black widow spider, the interval is about one hour.

The moulting process in all species of spiders is the most trying stage in their existence. In preparation for the ordeal, the black widow spider refrains from eating for several days before the event and is not tempted, as we have observed, either by domestic flies or any other of the choice morsels which comprise its staple diet. We have observed the moulting process as performed in both laboratory and field, and upon occasions have noted that it resulted in the death of the spider involved. The moulting process—when it does not result in death to the spider—weakens it to such an extent that the creature finds it necessary to rest for a day or so before assuming normal activity.

To complete the data on the structure of the black widow spider, it is necessary to strike a comparison between the male and female. There are three essential distinguishing features, the first of which concerns their relative size and color pattern. The male black widow spider ranges from a third to a little over half the length of the female; and in color, the male *L. mactans* shows an even more striking dissimiliarity. Very likely he will have four vertical stripes running along the side of his abdomen, a dark band down the middle of the front part of his body, and another, but of different design, along the mid section of his back. Like his spouse, he may have the yellow, orange, or red hourglass symbol beneath the abdomen, but in this case the marking sometimes tends to be dull and hardly recognizable. The fairly long and slender legs of the male—when seen under the magnifying lens—instead of each being all of one color are usually composed of alternate dark and light particles. While the color scheme of the male exhibits considerable variation, and specimens are occasionally found which are almost black, the typical color pattern is actually dark brown combined with a creamish hue.

Another difference between the male and female spider concerns their sexual characteristics. In the latter, the external opening of the reproductive organs is situated on the underside of the abdomen near its front or base, and in the middle line of the body. This cavity is termed the epignyum and is often of complicated structure, being composed of a number of distinct parts. More intricate still, however, are her internal reproductive organs, consisting of the ovaries, the oviducts, the vagina, and one or more pouches, termed the spermathecae, for the reception of the seminal fluid at the time of mating.

The internal reproductive organs of the male open on the underside of the abdomen at its base, which aperture serves as an outlet to emit the semen, but the external portion of his sexual apparatus presents a unique situation. The intromittent organ, which in almost all species of animals is found in close proximity to the testes, in the present instance is located in another portion of the body —the tips of the leg-like feelers. In the female, the pedipalpi are approximately even along their entire length, while in the male they end in an enlargement. The bulb of each of the two feelers in the male black widow appears to be nothing more than a plain black knob. Possession of these terminal endings or the lack of them determines the sex of the spider; and when present they render dual service. Indeed, so complicated is the construction of these comparatively tiny attachments, having (as Comstock has pointed out) as many as forty-four different parts, and so much do they differ in the various species, that taxonomists have used them as an aid in the classification of spiders.

The typical preparation for the mating process is performed in the following manner: Sometimes before the act of coition, the male spider spins a delicate skein of silk. This may depend from a dry leaf, a piece of bark, the surface of a smooth stone, or the thick, basic part of the permanent web. The seminal fluid is then deposited on this tiny napkin of silk, the secretion emanating from the opening of the reproductive organs beneath the abdomen. Then with one or the other of his pedipalpi, the spider dips therein and stores up the vital substance in the knobbed terminal ending. It is retained there until pairing takes place.

The relative quantity and potency of their poisons presents the third and last fundamental difference between the male and the female of the black widow species. While both possess poison glands and fangs, the sacs of the male have a capacity of approximately one third to one half that of the female. Also of note is the fact that the venom pouches of the female at all stages are opaque and filled with poison, while in the matured male they are translucent and are usually devoid of venom. Actually the sacs of the female increase in size—and the venom in strength—with maturity, while in the male the situation is just the reverse, for with adulthood his poison equipment becomes atrophied and inactive. This is true to the extent that it tends to be ineffective even when used on diminutive insect prey. Indeed, so weak and meagre in quantity is the venom of the male at all periods of his life that his bite is incapable of causing any serious injury to a human being, which fact is all the more strange since we know that his spouse's poison, drop for drop, exceeds the potency of rattlesnake venom.

The classification of the black widow spider begins with the question as to how she gained her popular name of "black widow." We know that, comparatively speaking, it is only within recent years that this title became attached to her. This ebony spider has, until of late, been graced by many and various, appellations. The Indians of California called her Po-ko-moo, and throughout various parts of the United States she—on account of manifold inherent characteristics—has sailed under various popular names, including "the hourglass spider," "the southern spider," "the red spotted spider," "the long-legged spider," "the deadly spider," "the T-spider," "the poison lady," "the shoe-button spider," "the poison spider," and "the black spider." The last name has become a descriptive term in black widow spider literature. With the turn of the century, however, the name "black widow" came into general use, and by the year 1912 even the great Comstock felt himself justified in perpetuating the title.

"Black widow" has been seized upon by popular writers who assert that the name is most appropriate by reason of the "fact" that after mating "she invariably eats the male." The popular belief, however, that once the nuptial functions are at an end the male serves as an inevitable gustative sacrifice is a fallacy not to be condoned. That the act is sometimes consummated is not to be denied, but not to the extent that she can be deservedly singled out as a mariticidal "widow." Her record as a husband head-huntress does not compare with that of certain other creatures of Arachnida such as the scorpion, the tarantula, and the trap-door spider. She eats her spouse after mating, yes, but only when in direst hunger. The term "black widow" has nevertheless become so firmly established in the minds of the lay public that it will require more than a denial of experts to displace it in popular fancy.

We shall now consider the history of how she obtained

her present scientific name of *Latrodectus mactans*. Beginning with *Aranea mactans* (which title Fabricus gave her in 1775), the black widow has been known severally as *L. formidabilis*, *L. perfidus*, *L. variolus*, *L. intersector*, *L. dotatus*, *L. apicallis*, *Tetragnatha zorilla*, *Theridium verecundum*, *Theridion lineatum*, and *T. carolinum*. Jaeger in his *Dictionary of Latin Combining Forms Used in Zoölogical Names* states that *Latrodectus* is derived from *latro*, a robber; and *dect(o)*, biting; hence, *Latrodectus*, a biting robber. *Mactans* is a Latin word meaning *murderous*. Hence a murderous biting robber.

This background enables us to place this spider in all her categories, from the phylum to the species. She belongs to the phylum *Arthropoda*, which, as previously stated, includes the insects, crabs, lobsters, millipedes and scorpions. She is a member of the class *Arachnida*, which embraces the spiders, scorpions, daddy-long-legs, mites and certain other less familiar forms. She is of the order *Araneida*, which comprises only the spiders. The spiders differ from the remaining members of the class *Arachnida* in that they possess an unsegmented abdomen joined to the cephalothorax by a slender stalk. The order is divided into two superfamilies, the *Avicularioidea* and *Argiopoidea*. The first is represented in the United States by two families, the *Aviculariidae*, which takes in the so-called tarantula and trap-door spiders, and the *Atypidae*, which is composed of a small number of tarantula-like spiders. The second superfamily, the *Argiopoidea*, to which the black widow spider belongs, contains the remaining twenty-eight families represented in the United States. Their distinguishing marks are that the claw of the chelicerae projects more or less downward, and that all except one of its members have either a single pair of book lungs or none at all. The black widow is of the family Theridiidae, or, as popularly known, the comb-footed spiders. All are noted for their tendency to spin irregular, coarsely-woven webs, from which they hang, like monkeys, belly upward. They have eight eyes and three tarsal claws. In addition to this distinguishing characteristic, the hind pair of legs is comb footed. The black widow is a member of the dangerous genus of this family, *Latrodectus*, which in various species may be found the world over. They are conspicuous in that the females are the largest in *Theridiidae*, the lateral eyes are widely separated, and the abdomen is globe shaped. And lastly, she is of the species *mactans*.

In recapitulation, the black widow belongs to the phylum *Arthropoda*, the class *Arachnida*, the order *Araneida*, the superfamily *Argiopoidea*, the family *Theridiidae*, the genus *Latrodectus*, and the species *mactans*.

Chamberlin and Ivie point out that not all adult females of the species *mactans* are precisely alike in color markings, or in relative length of legs. Their findings show that the species *mactans* may be divided into three varieties and that each tends to have its zone of habitation; namely, the eastern and central states, the southwestern states, and all states west of the Rocky Mountains. One of these varieties may have a red spot on the back above the spinnerets, or that color may extend as a band along the dorsal part of the spider; another may have a red streak just above the spinnerets, and also a small white mark on the anterior end; the third (referred to most in recent literature) is inevitably without color marks on the upper side of the abdomen, the whole dorsum being done in black. A perfect color pattern in the black widow presents the design of the red hourglass beneath the abdomen; a less perfect one shows her to be provided only with two or three small spots in this location; and imperfect or erratic specimens may be lacking in any marks whatsoever.

A thorough scientific knowledge of the spider is unnecessary in the instruction of laymen. It is vital, however, to know that all of the varieties of *L. mactans* have in common several visible tell-tale characteristics. They all weave coarse, irregular webs, possess eight wiry legs, and have a dominant coloring of shiny black. A bright colored mark of some shape may usually be found on the under side or, less frequently, on the upper side of her abdomen. With this general knowledge as to her markings, one will have little trouble in identifying her, and, in this connection, a more widespread recognition on the part of the public should lead to a steady decimation of the black widow horde.

14. The Life Cycle of the Black Widow Spider

~~~~~~

IT IS necessary, in order to comprehend certain characteristics of the black widow spider, to familiarize ourselves with the creature's entire life cycle. First, it is known that the male black widow spider takes the initative in the mating nuptials. This is not an assertion of masculine authority but is by permission only, as may be conjectured when we take into account the fact that he is far inferior to his spouse in size and fighting power. The male upon reaching maturity deserts his own abode and starts wandering about in search of a mate. His passionate quest is uninterrupted by less important issues, and comes to fruition only when he locates, hanging belly upward in some spider copse, a female of *L. mactans*.

When once she has been discovered, the dwarfish Lochinvar steps up and onto the foot of her webbed nest, and by palpitating his abdomen causes the entire web to vibrate. His is a dangerous mission, for if the female is not ready for his amatory advances, there may not be any reciprocating vibrations; and in the latter case it behooves the male to be careful with his overtures. If the female is not ready for coition, she lures the male within striking distance, and pounces upon and binds him in a mummy-like casket of web, subsequently feasting upon his life juices. If, on the other hand, he finds her in readiness to have her eggs fertilized, there is a mutual exchange of vibrations, after which the male cautiously picks his way up to her boudoir. There the wooing continues, and she becomes his voluntary prisoner in a loosely spun webbed envelope. The generative process is completed when the male applies the spring-like apparatus of either palpus to the genital opening of the female, following which she easily severs the threads that symbolically prove her subservience to her lord and master. Once the tiny spouse has served his natural purpose, his larger mate, unless suffering the pangs of hunger, allows him to go his way in peace.

The fertilized eggs quickly develop within the body of the black widow, and it takes on a swollen appearance. When the moment arrives for the deposition of the eggs, which is usually at night, she may be found hanging in a perpendicular position with head and forelegs upward. The pregnant spider then begins a swaying motion which is accomplished by pulling her body forward with her legs. With the continuation of this rhythmic movement, and as her body rocks to and fro, the genital flap in the abdomen opens and closes repeatedly. When the muscular exertion reaches the proper pitch, the spherical, butter-colored, ball-like eggs are, with each operation, forced out into a cup of webbed silk which was prepared in anticipation of the event. The webbed receptacle hangs upside down, and, from the spider's position, it appears to a casual observer that she is clinging to its rim. As the eggs are forced outward, gradually piling up and adhering to the silk, they seem "to be forced into an expanding, gelatin-like film. . . ." In order to expel the last ones, she must exert considerable effort, and her abdomen, which was formerly dangerously distended, becomes wrinkled and contracted, shrinking to less than half its former size. The egg sac contains from twenty-five to a thousand of the single globules.

The next operation of the black widow is to enclose the eggs in a webbed sac. This she does by sealing up the cup. Turning her spinnerets until they are close to the eggs, she emits a viscid silk and with her rear legs covers the open end of the cup with loose strands, finally working the filament over the entire mass. This is repeated again and again until the egg sac is completed, by which time it has assumed the shape of a marble. Shortly after this, the film surrounding the eggs appears to evaporate, and they are free to roll about in the cocoon. The egg sac approximates the tip-of-the-thumb size and at first is white, but from exposure to the air it soon becomes tan or yellowish. It is watertight, is of sufficient toughness to isolate its inmates from all insect predators, and provides the former with a hollowed-sphere shelter from the elements. The fabric, while insulating the eggs from the glaring sunlight, nevertheless serves as a conductor of the necessary warmth for proper incubation. In point of time the deposition of the eggs and the construction of the cocoon consumes no less than an hour, and under certain conditions this stretches out into as much as three hours.

Upon the completion of the egg sac, which is held in position in her nest by cables of web, the black widow exhibits the usual maternal instinct and may be seen hovering in close proximity to it in her characteristic position of back down, belly up, and legs clinging to the web. During this period she exhibits a marked attitude of pugnacity, and if sufficiently provoked will dart swiftly in the direction of any agent that disturbs the web. In an experiment whereby the egg sac was shifted to another portion of the web, we have noted the tedious process by which the spider manipulates it back into a position of her own choosing. We have also noted that when the web is between two boulders, at midday the spider may convey the egg sac into the upper and sunny portion of her nest; and with the sun's setting, work the cocoon against one of the boulders. During the long night the eggs are incubated from the warmth retained in the rock.

Meanwhile life is being developed within the egg sac. Inside the cocoon the young shed their skin for the first time, a necessary process before they are able to feed, and upon occasions they have been known to go through their second moult therein. The time they remain within the egg sac ranges from about four days in summer to about one month during cold weather. When the moment finally arrives for their emergence, they make one or more holes in the closely woven fabric, and then, singly, squeeze through and out onto the web of their parent, who is inevitably within watchful distance of them. In the tip-of-the-thumb size world which has been theirs they leave behind the discarded skins, or egg shells.

As they cling in a beautiful cluster to their parent's web—their chitin-covered bodies becoming toughened by the outer atmosphere—the lives of the spiderlings are threatened from several quarters. The younglings, who are much too frail to snare insect victims, feed upon one another, but an even greater hazard is faced in the cannibalistic propensities of the ferocious mother. We have observed the latter's tactics many times. First she thrusts out one long, jointed leg, which after resting momentarily upon a tiny creature, transports the spiderling to the maw of its parent. The action is mechanical, and within a few minutes scores of the spiderlings serve to satiate the gastronomical lusts of the unnatural mother. Those which survive these dangers are beset by predaceous creatures, including insects of various types and spiders of both the sedentary and hunting varieties. But, despite these dangers, a majority of the spiderlings usually survive the perils of infancy.

There are several means by which the survivors disperse to various portions of the continent of their origin. The most commonly known mediums of spider travel are furnished by the inventions of mankind. Black widow spiders are often transported, as unwanted passengers, in automobiles, freight trains, and steamships. Many automobile travelers unknowingly transport the dangerous spiders several hundred miles, or mayhap, clear across the country. Traveling in box cars, the creatures are often carried from one town to another and from state to state, and in some instances spend their lives in riding about and propagating the species in divers localities. It is a known fact that *Latrodectus* has invaded the Hawaiian Islands, where formerly this genus did not exist. In all probability the original specimens were transported there by boat.

The young black widow, as is usual with some other species, sometimes climbs the stalk of a plant, from which position she lets out many filmy strands of silk, which float upward and outward, lifting the little one's abdomen.

In a short while the balloon of web thus formed exerts a pull that flaunts the spiderling almost loose from its moorings. More gossamer strands float out upon the breeze, until finally the creature is lifted up and carried out over the terrain toward an unknown destination. Her maiden flight may end only a short distance from the parental nest, or an air current may take her far away and deposit her in strange environment.

In another instance the spiderling may wander, afoot, only a few yards distant from her birthplace. The location she chooses as the site of a permanent abode may, if out of doors, be a boulder or a clump of grass. In such case her companions in home-building likewise may construct similar nests to the right and left and across from her, resulting in a formation which, with the maternal parent's abode in the center, may be thought of as radiating out like the spokes of a wheel. With each successive season, circle overlaps circle. Should this occur within an uncultivated field, with the grass, the weeds, and the brush growing uncut year after year, the area—as instances have proved—may cover many hundreds of square feet and become a veritable breeding ground for black widow spiders.

Wherever the spiderling locates, she there constructs a webbed dwelling. In the beginning, because of her tiny size and needs comparatively less than those of the parent, the strands of silk thus provided are few and short of length. With the passing of time, however—should her location provide the space—the webbed nest may be enlarged to a three-foot diameter. Time and again, in consequence of the ravages of time, the elements, and the insect destroyers, the maturing widow will find it necessary to furnish repairs to her original work. On occasion, too, she may as a result of some annoyance desert her abode and move to another site, there to construct a similar nest.

In a description of the manner in which this creature builds her abode, let us suppose, for example, that she intends to spin her web in the corner of a basement. First, she climbs up the wall for a distance of a foot or more, and possibly an inch from where the two sides join to form the corner. Once set, her spinnerets emit a large number of minute, viscid threads, which adhere to the surface of the wall and are known scientifically as the "attachment disc." Thus anchored, she lets herself downward by means of a web which is spun out from her rear and fastened to the floor whereon she alights. She then climbs up the guy line, at the same time spinning out more web. As an alternate procedure the spider may drop and swing herself a short distance below and to the opposite wall, or otherwise may put forth a strand of web to be caught up by the air currents and flung to the opposite wall, where, because of its sticky texture, it adheres. With this done she will pull the thread tight with her hind legs and attach it to the surface on which she is standing.

Once this bridge has been completed, many additional possibilities are provided. It may be strengthened by her passing back and forth over it, each time adding a dragline. She may fasten a thread one-half, three-quarters, or a full inch below this, and then, crawling up to the bridge, walk across it. As this latter action takes place the creature is letting out a dragline which is kept free of the bridge by the manipulations of one of her legs. After reaching the other side she crawls down to whatever position is deemed desirable, pulls the cable taut, and fastens it by means of the attachment disc. More likely, however, she will select a position near the apex of the web, and there spin an extra number of strands to form a sort of pocket. This would constitute the inner castle of her abode. Taken as a whole, however, the completed domicile manifests *little design other than a zig-zag criss-cross net work.* With the accumulation of dust, it takes on the *coarse, dirty appearance* so descriptive of the black widow's unspiderlike lack of art.

It is in such a nest as described above that the spiderling grows into adulthood. While yet in the egg sac, she has passed through the first moult. She started out as a tiny, opalescent white creature without any dark spots on her body. But with the second moult (which may or may not occur while in the cocoon) and succeeding through the third, fourth, and fifth, the growing spider takes on various markings. The hourglass symbol can be detected while she is still in the early spiderling stage. The male and female (up to and through the fifth moulting, at which point the former becomes matured) develop in about the same way. The general appearance of the male is marked by four perpendicular, dark-colored stripes on each side of the abdomen, a band along the fore part of his body, and another of a different pattern down the mid-section of his back. These physical characteristics, together with his size, cause the male to look not unlike his sisters of the same brood. The female offspring are, however, unlike him in that they go through two extra moultings before reaching maturity. The sixth and seventh moultings of the female, aside from causing her to become larger, produce decided changes in coloring, the patterns all merging into each other until she becomes soot black, with the hourglass symbol on her abdomen and perhaps a crimson spot on the upper side of the hinder portion.

The figures five and seven represent, respectively, the number of moultings ordinarily necessary before the male and female attain maturity. An abundance of food and optimum temperature will reduce the number of moultings of the male from five to three, and those of the female, from seven to six. On the other hand, should less favorable conditions obtain—thus resulting in slower growth—the male may be forced to go through as many as six, and the female, eight, or even nine moults. Thus the number of moults experienced by the male and female are, respectively, from three to six, and from six to nine.

There are three other phases in the life and habits of *L. mactans.* The first concerns the numerical ratio of males to females; the second revolves around the time element required for the female to complete her life cycle; and the third concerns the longevity of the black widow spider.

The first, the ratio of sexes, represents the most difficult problem, for it is well-nigh impossible to differentiate between the sexes until the spiderlings are one-third matured. "Of one series consisting of 55 individuals reared in the laboratory," according to one report, "31 males reached maturity; and of 119 individuals observed out of doors under natural conditions, only 21 were males." In another series comprising eighty-two individuals matured in the laboratory, there were thirty-seven males and forty-five females; and of 153 individuals observed in the wild, there were twenty-seven males. A legitimate calculation would be that while under laboratory conditions the ratio of males and females reaching maturity is about equal, in the open (and under natural conditions) the number of females that reach full growth outnumber the males. This is undoubtedly due in large part to the female's ability to hold her own against natural enemies and at the same time obtain her sustenance more readily than the males.

The second phase, the length of time for the female to grow from an egg to an adult, is determined to a certain extent by environmental factors. Under the most favorable conditions of food, temperature, and humidity, it requires at least two, and more likely three or four, months. On account of the popular belief—supported by natural laws—that the black widow species is in greater abundance during the late summer and fall, at that season the newspapers herald the fact that an unwelcome visitor is present in the community. Daily items furnish testimony that the creatures have been discovered about the attic or basement. Boys at play on the vacant lot, gardeners at work on the shrubbery and lawn, and naturalists in the field continually report finding black widow spiders, many of which are killed or collected for experimental purposes.

The widespread belief that the dangerous black widow is more abundant during the period of summer and early fall is also supported by numerous medical reports. The latter record that a majority of spider-bite cases occur from July to October, inclusive, which means—on the four-months basis of growth from egg to maturity—that the adult female spiders in these months were in the egg stage either in April, May, June, or the first days in July. This very fact, however, is but a warning that care should also be exercised during the months named, for it is at this time that the matured female may be found incubating the egg sacs. As we heretofore pointed out, it is during the incubating period that the old beldame is prone to bite. Thus, while the black widow is more prolific during the hottest months of the year, actually she may be found all the year around, and her victims have really boxed the calendar.

Lastly, we shall concern ourselves with the longevity of the black widow, and this may be calculated from several standpoints. When a brood emerges in the late spring or early summer, it will, on the four-months basis, reach maturity before cold weather arrives. More likely, however, it will leave off egg-laying until the following spring, and will die a natural death some days later, which allots to it a life span of only one year. On the other hand, those spiders which come from the cocoon in late July and August do not reach maturity by the advent of cold weather. They accordingly spend the winter in the same immature state and, because of the scarcity of insect food and adverse weather conditions, their normal development is seriously retarded. It is not until the arrival of the warm days, with the added consequence of an abundance of insect food, that these late-comers reach maturity and develop the power to reproduce young. Broods such as this naturally are fitted to a total existence of at least a year and a half. Further, laboratory tests have proved that female black widows may live through a second and even a third summer, thus alloting to them a life span of over two years. This, together with the fact that a matured female may spin and fill a total of nine egg sacs—the interval between the successive cocoons varying from about one week to four months, each sac containing from twenty-five to a thousand eggs—indicates a potential increase, year by year, that is staggering.

15. Diet of the Black Widow Spider

〜〜〜〜〜〜〜〜〜〜〜〜〜〜〜〜〜〜〜〜〜〜〜〜〜〜〜〜〜〜〜〜〜〜〜〜〜〜〜

HAVING traced the complete life cycle of the black widow spider, let us examine in detail another phase of her existence which is most significant in relation to controlling her numbers. This phase has to do with how she obtains her prey and what constitutes her diet.

We shall first begin with a consideration of the means whereby she obtains food. Nature has equipped the black widow spider with three major weapons with which to bring about the destruction of her prey. Since she is a sedentary and not a hunting spider, the nest wherein she keeps the vigil, the snare, constitutes an integral part of the process used in obtaining food. Although this coarse, permanent web is not particular viscid in quality, it nevertheless causes inadvertent insect visitors to become temporarily entangled. In most instances the moment a creature sets foot therein, it becomes enfettered with silk, its subsequent struggles causing it to become even more hopelessly entangled. And the vain struggles to free itself act as a boomerang in yet another way, for they serve to inform the black widow of the intruder's presence. Actually, when compared with some other species of spiders, *L. mactans* does not possess an acute discerning tactile sense, at times not being able, as experiments have demonstrated, to differentiate between the buzzing of a fly caught in her nest and a synthetic vibration of the web by a person rotating a stalk of grass therein. If the intruder proves to be a palpitating insect, she proceeds to make short work of it. After it has been captured and quelled, the spider may permit the morsel to remain trussed up at the location of the kill; or on the other hand, it may be conveyed to the pocket-part of her nest where, at her leisure, she devours it. When once the life juices have been removed, the black widow—as a gesture of tidiness—cuts all points of attachment between the web and the body-shell, permitting the latter to fall free amid the husks of previous victims.

Next in importance to the snare itself is a webbed weapon of quite a different quality. This substance comes from different spigots of her spinnerets, and is called the swathing film. The gluey material is only used on the struggling victim in special cases, for *L. mactans* tends to economize her powers and allows no more play than is necessary to bring about the desired ends. This shroud of swathing is a wrapping which gives to the victim literally a mummified appearance, and could not be applied without the use of the last joint—the tarsus—of her fourth pair of legs, which is covered with spine-like hairs that resemble the teeth of a comb. This comb is used for flinging the silk, in its liquid state, over the entangled prey. The black widow proceeds in this operation by backing up to her insect victim. When within range she extends a freshly spun strand of viscid silk with one or both hind legs, and, with the prisoner kicking to free itself, attempts to tie down the thrashing appendages. Should the ensnared prey appear particularly turbulant, she ejects from her spinnerets large, viscous quick-drying droplets, the properties of which are similar to rubber cement. Once entangled in these, escape for the victim becomes well-nigh impossible, and the spider goes about the usual routine in disposing of the unfortunate prisoner.

Inasmuch as some insects have more vitality than others, the spider frequently finds it necessary to augment this treatment by the use of her greatest weapon—the fangs. In such case the black widow nips the creature, injecting a certain amount of venom, upon which the victim struggles violently in the throes of death. These tremors become progressively weaker, and within a few moments cease altogether.

The black widow, being possessed of such an efficient assemblage of equipment for predatory purposes, is thus enabled to subdue a variety of creatures for her sustenance. We have, upon numerous occasions, fed black widow spiders on sowbugs, the latter having been procured from beneath discarded pieces of corrugated sheetiron, old timbers, and other rubbish. They are small creatures belonging to the class Crustacea, are from a quarter- to a half-inch in length, have hard shells covering the upper part of the body, and possess a multiplicity of minute legs projecting from the under parts. If one will introduce a sowbug into a container with a black widow spider, it will be noted that the latter needs bring into play only a minimum of her arms paraphernalia in order to overcome such a docile victim. She, in purely routine manner, ties it down with a few strands of webbing, and in due time withdraws its life juices.

As another example of her food-getting proficiency, we have a typical case of black widow versus clear-winged grasshopper. Upon inserting the latter into the jar which housed the spider, we witnessed a procedure somewhat different from the above mentioned. The spider, after backing up to the entangled grasshopper, quickly swerved away, seemingly for the purpose of gauging the calibre of her bulky captive. Her strategy soon became apparent. With the grasshopper's repeated struggles, it bound itself tighter and tighter, to a degree that its motions became somewhat diminished. At the moment of the victim's greatest weakness, the spider rushed upward with lightning speed, and in a short period succeeded in tying the creature securely.

Upon another occasion we, by taking a cue from a fellow naturalist, offered up for slaughter a half dozen domestic flies. Simultaneously they became entangled in the web which clouded the inside of the jar. The black widow quickly back-pedaled to the scene of mass entanglement and was on the verge of subduing one of the flies when another set up a wing vibration, attracting her attention in its direction. Reconsidering, the spider backed up to it, but before she had time to put the quietus to its actions, another and another of the flies began struggling to wrest themselves from the web which held them prisoners. The black widow accordingly rushed from one fly to the other, presenting a marvelous exhibition of speed and ability. For a period of about two minutes she was as busy as an executive trying to answer a deskful of telephones all ringing at the same time. Finally, however, by judicious use of both silk and fangs, she succeeded in quieting the struggles of her victims.

Specimens of *L. mactans* will feed upon the sowbug, grasshopper, and domestic fly not only in the laboratory;

they are also included in the staple diet in her natural surroundings. During our field investigations we have found in the webs of black widow spiders carcasses of victims including the alfalfa butterfly, the codling moth, the beet leaf hopper, the black vine weevil, the snowy tree cricket, the gooseberry fruit fly, the vinegar fly, the squash bug, the matured tomato worm, the cutworm, the nocturnal moth, and the vegetable weevil. These creatures do not attain to large size and are easily subdued by the spider. On the other hand, we have frequently observed the carcasses of other species, some many times the size of the black widow, within the nest. Among these may be mentioned the centipede, the scorpion, and the Jerusalem cricket. Because our observations in this wise have been limited largely to California, from San Diego County on the south to as far north as Marin County, this list represents only a local picture of black widow provender. In other portions of the country there are species of the classes Crustacea, Arachnida, Diplopoda, Chilopoda and Hexapoda not native to California, and from these the black widow spider, who is not too fastidious as to her provender, would choose many for her victuals. Actually, we have learned from our investigations that this spider feeds upon creatures ranging from small to large, nonvenomous to venomous, sluggish to lightning swift.

As one might easily discover from visible evidences in the web and deposited beneath, *Latrodectus* eats every sort of insect, but the exact number consumed by a single specimen can only be accurately appraised by keeping the feeding records of those reared in the laboratory. Life records of one specimen totaled 240 domestic flies, three grasshoppers, and two garden spiders; another, 197 domestic flies, seven sowbugs and a small centipede; a third, 255 domestic flies, twelve sowbugs and three grasshoppers; a fourth, 163 domestic flies, two nocturnal moths, one grasshopper, and one Jerusalem cricket; and a fifth, 173 domestic flies, twenty-one vinegar flies, and three grasshoppers.

The black widow spider nevertheless can, despite her gormandizing nature, go for long periods without food. We have harbored specimens—without giving them access to food—three and four months at a time. During this interval each spider's abdomen, which at the beginning was nicely rounded and of a satiny texture, had dwindled and shrunk like a deflated balloon, and appeared to have lost some of its former luster. In one instance when—in scientific pursuit—we deprived a specimen of food, we found at the end of a six-month period that the creature, upon being teased, exhibited her former activity. Upon another occasion we learned—unwittingly—of the remarkable ability of the black widow to withstand famine. One day in 1935 we had occasion to transfer to another location some twenty jars which contained specimens of black widows. Each of the containers was labeled with the date on which its occupant had been placed there. Through an unfortunate oversight one of the jars, from being placed in a dark corner, was overlooked in the transition, and remained undiscovered for a period of nine months. When the container turned up in the course of a general cleaning, however, we found the spider occupant, although greatly shrunken, still alive. Upon being supplied with food, it slowly recovered.

We therefore see that the diet of *L. mactans* is based upon a "come-what-may" menu, since she feeds upon a variety of insects and sundry creatures. Our investigations and the literature of the subject reveal, in fact, that this spider's larder is adaptable to such food as her residential locality provides. We have shown, too, that when food is abundant the black widow exhibits a glutton's capacity, but, on the other hand, should there be a scarcity of forage, she adapts herself accordingly. Her power to fast for long periods is an outstanding characteristic. The above-mentioned propensities thus enable L. mactans to thrive where there is an abundance of insect food, to remain active when there is a scarcity, and even to remain alive over long periods under systematic starvation.

16. Home-Building Sites

~~~~~~

THE SECOND phase of the black widow spider's existence concerns nest-building sites, including the climatic and topographical conditions under which she exists. We —as well as persons interviewed by us—have found black widow spiders living under unusual conditions. Once, while one of us was ringing the doorbell at the house of an acquaintance, a black widow spider emerged, seemingly from nowhere, within three inches of the instrument. The hand was quickly drawn away. Subsequent scrutiny revealed that the spider's cable of web was stretched from the bottom portion of the door, upward to the eaves of the roof. Looking closely, we could discern the spider's nest. As our gaze became centered upon her, the creature, having descended to within six inches of the base of her cable, reversed her direction and quickly returned to her abode. At the moment we were at a loss as to whether to kill the spider or to capture her alive and add her to our growing menagerie of creatures of the Arachnida. To leave her unmolested was, of course, out of the question. The next visitor, or mayhap the owners of the house, themselves, might not prove so fortunate. Finally, we decided to take possession of the spider, and forthwith secured a paper bag from a nearby grocery.

Upon returning to the scene we discovered that the black widow spider had again emerged from her lair and was halfway down the cable. With skill born of much experience, we were enabled to entice the spider into the container.

At another time, during the late summer when the maintenance crew of a certain grammar school were preparing the grounds for the fall semester, one of the workmen discovered a black widow spider and cocoons on the underside of a bench. He immediately went to the foreman and told him of his discovery. The workmen procured long sticks, and, after setting the bench on end, proceeded to smash the adult female spider and her potential broods. With this accomplished, one of the men—as an after thought—examined a second bench and found himself confronted with an identical situation. The remaining benches were then investigated, with the result that at least a score of the matured females with their egg sacs were brought into view. The laborers continued their work of extermination—with additional spiders being continually discovered—until at last the foreman, foreseeing the hopelessness of it all, give the order to cease, promising to obtain services of professional exterminators.

A similar case was retailed to us by a person who supervises the paint sprayers in a furniture manufacturing concern. The raw furniture when needed is rolled from the warehouse to the spraying room, which adjoins it. One day a workman in the act of so doing pulled open the drawer of a buffet and beheld therein a matured female black widow spider with two egg sacs. Subsequent investigation revealed that other pieces of furniture were abodes for these spiders. At first the workmen attacked the

venomous creatures with sticks, but the hopelessness of
this effort was seen with the continued moving of other
pieces of furniture. Actually, the warehouse turned out to
be a veritable breeding place for black widow spiders.
Efforts have been made to exterminate them in wholesale fashion, but no satisfactory procedure toward this
result has yet been worked out. The only successful
method has been the slow, crude process of using a stick.
The workmen at this place use the utmost care and dili-
gence, and it is due to this fact that no one has yet been
victimized by the dangerous spiders.

From personal observations, correspondence, conversations, and the literature of the subject, we can report that
the black widow spider has been found not only in a
variety of locations but existing under manifold conditions. Our inquiries disclose that she has been discovered
in a surprising number of man-made structures, including
human habitations. Uncounted numbers have been found
under the seats of privies; in the darkened corners of garages, chicken coops, and rabbit pens; in basements, storage
buildings, and barns; behind shutters, in rain spouts, and
within bundles of old letters; beneath shelves, in book-
stacks, shoe boxes, and pump houses; in closets, cellars,
tool sheds, and piles of automobile casings; under board
walks, in man-holes, metal waste containers, and smoke
houses; in piles of tincans, on rafters, in unused flower
pots and meter boxes, under steps and in tile roofs; about
culverts, in outsheds, on porches, under eaves, and on old
boards; in openings under concrete walks, piles of gunny-
sacks, sewer pipes, and box cars; among loose bricks, in
pine packing boxes, and in reed baskets; behind store dis-
plays, under loose flagstones, on undersides of plant tables

in greenhouses, and about stove pipes in summer storage.

Our investigations show that she has been found variously in the fields and out of doors: in wheat, oat, and barley shocks; in eroded granite and beneath loose stones; in bundles of fodder and stacks of hay, between bales of cotton, and in cotton stalks; in post holes, tree stumps, hollows of trees, and under old logs; in bushes, clumps of grass, newly cleared ground, and the uncultivated earth in fence corners; in rock piles and fissures of the earth, on ears of corn, in vines about the veranda, and in prickly pear cactus; in tomato and asparagus fields, vineyards, and deserted bird's nests, and across abandoned squirrel, prairie dog, and gopher burrows.

Our research reveals that *Latrodectus* has also been found in unusual places. Specimens have been discovered in the sleeve of a work shirt, under a rocking chair, in a shoe, in the radiator at the head of a bed, in the bed itself, in milk bottles, behind books on the library shelf, in a hat, behind a picture frame, beneath a bath tub, inside a cuckoo clock, in a suit case, in an old well, under the back cushion seat of an automobile, in a typewriter box, in the back pocket of a pair of overalls, under a wash basin and within the framework of a scarecrow.

In brief, while the black widow spider's hiding places have been found most frequently to be under the seats of privies, the darkened corners of garages, basements, and attics, it is known that she builds her nest practically anywhere that facilities exist for attaching a web.

In addition, this spider has not only been discovered in various sites, but has also been found living under varied climatic and topographical conditions. Observations show that she can stand fairly cold weather. Within the vicinity of Denver, she has been observed during December, January, February, and March as well as throughout the remainder of the year. D'Amour, Becker, and Van Riper report that the degree of activity shown by *Latrodectus* during the winter months appears to depend upon the temperature. If it is warm, the individuals captured behave as they do in the summer; if cold, they are more or less torpid. They state that during the winter the black widow is found in all of the common places, with not the slightest evidence extant that additional precautions against the cold weather have been provided. Many of those found under stones and in trash heaps are minus webs of any kind. In one locality, during the month of December, after heavy snows had resulted in cold nights, a live specimen was plucked from the bottom of a pile of tumbleweeds. A half-dozen black widow spiders froze to death in an unheated room, but only after a sudden cold snap had brought the temperature down to ten degrees below zero (Fahrenheit).

In sharp contrast, we have found black widow spiders in locations where the heat of summer is intense, such as Imperial Valley of southern California, the country about Needles, California, various areas of the Mojave and Colorado deserts, and in certain portions of Death Valley. During the summer and early autumn the temperature of these localities often rises far above the hundred-degree mark. The black widow favors a dark, cool location but is not averse to the sunlight as is the tarantula, which creature will die if exposed for only a few minutes. Investigations make it clear that warmth does not retard the growth of the black widow, but, on the contrary, enables her to thrive and increase. A warm winter enables a larger number of females to survive; consequently, with the coming of spring and summer, they deposit their eggs and thus become more prolific.

The tremendous range of temperature in which the black widow may thrive brings up the question as to whether or not she does as well in widely divergent altitudes. Concerning this, the report of D'Amour, Becker, and Riper mentions that a majority of approximately 6,500 spiders collected for experimental purposes were obtained in the foothill country between Denver and Colorado Springs. This section of the country has an altitude of five thousand feet or more, but the report goes further in stating that black widow spiders were found in Estes Park at an altitude of seven thousand, that one specimen was discovered near Buffalo Park at eight thousand feet, and still another near the village of Estes, at an altitude of 8,200 feet.

Latrodectus has also been reported in regions paralleling the Gulf of Mexico and in communities along both the Atlantic and the Pacific Ocean. From our long residence in Los Angeles, we have had occasion to conduct personal investigations and to make inquiries concerning near-by settlements which are directly on the ocean front. Within these areas and in hearing distance of the breakers, the black widow spider is known to be abundant. We have observed many specimens in man-made structures such as garages, sheds, stores, offices, and dwelling houses, where they thrive with impunity despite gales, foggy atmosphere, and rains.

Other conditions to consider concerning the life and propagation of the spider have to deal with aridity (implying a comparative lack of insect foods), and heavy rainfall (resulting in an abundance of spider rations). That the black widow can exist in an arid region, depending for her food upon the few insects that the area provides, is attested by the fact that—to cite a few localities—specimens have been found in Death Valley, the semi-arid lands of the Yakima Valley in the state of Washington, and unirrigated sections of the Texas and Oklahoma panhandles, Nebraska and Wyoming, Montana and the Dakotas, Idaho and Nevada, Utah and New Mexico. Contrasted with this is the fact that the spider has been observed in areas where there is abundance of rainfall. In the densely foliaged sections of Medocino, Humboldt, and Del Norte counties of northern California, in central and east Texas, the delta country of Louisiana and Mississippi, and in certain of the humid parts of the Carolinas, eastern Tennessee, Florida, Georgia, and Alabama—to name only a few localities—the black widow spider is a permanent and conspicuous resident.

Thus it will be seen that the black widow is no respecter of climate or locality. She thrives where it is hot and where it is cold; and equally evident is the fact that her physical endurance and versatility enable her to thrive at altitudes from three hundred feet below sea level to more than eight thousand feet above. Studies show that while she prefers a dry climate to a wet one, the creature manages to survive in either. With such a liberal range in requirements, *Latrodectus* has thus been enabled to adjust her living habits to survive practically any condition which may exist in each of the forty-eight states.

17. Artificial Control

~~~~~~

SINCE the spider scare of 1934, men have made various attempts to work out a means of control for *Latrodectus mactans*. We have accordingly made a close study of all the methods put forward and present herewith the results of this painstaking review. There are only two practical paths toward control of an insect or arachnid menace: one is through the use of artificial, and the other by natural, means. The first involves the use of fumigants, sprays, pastes, or some sort of mechanical device which, when applied to the creatures, would result in wholesale destruction. The other concerns the utilization of some other species of creature (whether it be insect, reptile, or mammal) which would not be averse to feeding upon the black widow and (or) its eggs.

Many proposals looking toward control of this dangerous spider by artificial means have been set forth. The burning of trash piles, rubbish heaps, straw stacks, hay mounds, leaf piles and decayed vegetation accumulations has been advanced by many as a means to destroy the webs, the egg sacs and the adult female spiders. This is somewhat efficacious, but raises the objection of fire hazard. The argument has been set forth that, while fire would destroy the nest and cocoons, the adult spider would escape unscathed. Sensing the heat and flame, say these critics, the black widow could easily scurry away to safety, later to mate and produce more offspring.

There is a further proposal that the spider can be destroyed by drowning, sometimes with bland oil, but more often with water. This may result in destruction of the web, but obviously cannot harm the spider beyond forcing her to seek a new location. Water poured with sufficient quantity upon the egg sacs will break loose their webbed attachments to the nest, but owing to the waterproof qualities of the cocoon fabric, will result in no further damage. The black widow, washed down from her perch by the deluge, simply curls up in the characteristic spider fashion, and remains quiescent until the inconvenience is over. Water is a poor substance with which to attempt the destruction of a creature inured to desert cloudbursts.

Some authorities contend that the use of sprays loaded with undiluted creosote oil will take care of the black widow menace. The oil spraying method has in past years been recommended by both state and federal experimenters. Directions stated that the spray could best be applied with a bucket pump or compressed-air sprayer, and could be used in locations such as piles of brick or tile, stacks of old boards or logs, and in garages and the outdoor toilet. Proponents claim that the spray will kill if applied directly to the spider; and also that it exerts a repellent effect upon others. Controlled experiments, however, prove the erroneous character of this belief. All concerned have conceded that this material must be used with care, since it destroys vegetation, damages paint, and is irritating to the human skin. Moreover, the spray has been found impractical for this purpose with the three most potent ingredients—beechwood, carbolic acid, or crude coal-tar creosote. Laboratory tests show that one gram of creosote to a jar measuring six and a half inches in height and two and three quarter inches in diameter will prove fatal to a black widow spider in the same container, but that such high concentration cannot be developed in the open. Creosotes seems to be useless in combating the black widow spider in its natural habitat.

Other materials have in some quarters been highly praised, but all when subjected to scientific investigation fail in the one essential point: they don't kill the spider. When one gram of the substance was used in a jar six and one-half inches tall and two and three-quarters inches in diameter, with a matured, female black widow spider within the container, it was learned that acetone, antimony potassium tartrate, calcium chloride, sodium fluoride, sulphur, nitrobenzine, pine oil, pyrethrum powder, triorthocresyl phosphate, and Union garden spray all were ineffective.

Regarding the efforts mentioned above, it was found that any substance which would actually kill the spider must necessarily be used in such high concentration that the life and health of the user would be placed in jeopardy. It is inevitable that in using the highly toxic agents some measure will be inhaled, thereby injuring the health of the user. Those chemical agents which have proved the most effective, as cyanid, isoamyl, alcohol, and lethane, are therefore forbidden except under very special conditions. The health question, however, is but one of several factors to be considered. There is also the possibility of fire arising from sprays with mineral or kerosene bases and of explosive mixtures resulting from organic substances in friction with the atmosphere; and added to this is the possible corrosive, bleaching effect of the substance upon both plants and animals.

Sundry steam, fire, and electrical gadgets and manufactured formulae have been designed for the purpose of curtailing the propagation of the black widow, but in most instances these have proved either impractical or ineffective. In this category may be placed the commercial preparations which during recent years have been advanced as deterrents to the black widow. We have received the many advertisements, and have made it a point to purchase and use the heralded products, and in each instance the ingredients did not measure up to the claims as set forth in the label. Our experiments suggest that such preparations had not been tested to any appreciable degree on the black widow spider, although in all probability many of them had previously been used, and with telling effect, as insect exterminators.

Herein lies the germ of miscalculation so prevalent among merchants who—for quick profits—become temporary "scientists." Their mistake lay in placing the black widow spider in the category of insect. This is a very serious error. The black widow spider owns characteristics of hardihood which, in their combination, far excel those of many other creatures of Insecta and Arachnida. If she loses a leg, the member will be replaced by a new one. Because of her restricted diet of living-body juices, the black widow invariably ignores feeding poisons. A majority of the contact poisons fail to have any effect on her hard, chitinous body, and her breathing apparatus is well protected beneath her underside. Because of her slow respiratory requirements, many poisons of this nature (which are efficacious when used on common insects) are totally ineffective when used as a deterrent to the black widow. She is not known to suffer much from disease, only a few instances of fungi having been observed, and those on defunct specimens.

Serious recommendations, however, have been made toward control of the black widow spider. Following extensive experimental studies, Bogen and Loomis have shown that, on the score of effectiveness, cheapness, safety and simplicity, naphthalene is the best fumigant for small boxes, chests, and similar inclosed spaces. This is the commercial mothball material, to be used in amounts of two ounces to each cubic foot of space. Sulphur dioxide from sulphur candles—in the ratio of a pound of sulphur for every thousand cubic feet of space—left at least one hour in large, sealable chambers, and cyanide—in the ratio of three ounces for each thousand feet of storage space—are effective; but they must be used where the safety of human beings is assured. It has been recommended that kerosene be used in spraying. To increase the rapidity of its action, add a small amount—one to ten per cent of isoamyl alcohol, or the commercial organic compound lethane.

Actually, however, both fumigant and spray lack certain characteristics which, significantly, limit their services. No fumigant or repellent has been discovered that can be relied upon for use under houses or in privies. No spray that does not reach the spider can be effective, and the more thoroughly the spider is wet with the spray, the more certain and speedy is its death. With the materials that have been used, it has been found that spraying the empty portions of the web is without effect.

Thus, in view of the limitations in the use of chemical substances, other artifical measures have proved more effective in lessening the numbers of black widow spiders. It has been found advisable to attach hinges to the seat of the privy so that its underside may be periodically inspected for black widow spiders. The outbuildings should also be well lighted and finely screened. Newborn spiderlings may readily pass through ordinary screen, but this barrier will tend to keep out the insects upon which the black widow feeds. By restricting the creature's rations, therefore, one might readily compel her to vacate such a location and take up residence elsewhere.

It is desirable periodically to clear away all rubbish and waste material, whether in closets, the attic, basement, barn or the out-of-doors. The black widow spider may be found practically anywhere she can attach her web, and one should strive to leave her no advantage for home making. When one is engaged upon a foray of destruction against the black widow spider, and the locality is not bright and sunshiny, such as the interior of a garage, a flashlight is indispensable. It is also expedient to wear white clothing, with the bottoms of the trousers tucked into boots and the collar fastened tight. Under such conditions the spider could not creep or drop upon one's body and remain unseen.

The most effective artifical means of spider destruction are mechanical measures, such as the use of a fly swatter, shoe, broom, or stick. In wielding such weapons, extreme care must be exercised lest one brush against invisible strands of web and thus dislodge the spider. The weapon in use should be held at arm's length. Care should be taken in all cases to see that the spider is quickly killed. In addition, the egg sacs should be sought out and demolished. Care must be taken to see that the tiny spiders do not get an opportunity to escape from the cocoons and thus gain their freedom.

18. Natural Control

—wwwwwwwwwwwwwwwwwwwwwwwwwwwwwwwwwwwwwwwwwwwwwwwwwwwwww

THE QUEST for the natural enemy of the black widow. is a most important consideration which must not be overlooked. That this enemy exists is a certainty. The way of nature is for life to feed upon life to such an extent that no specific kind can increase beyond proportion so that it will become a major menace. The constant spreading of civilization, however, has in many instances interfered with the laws of nature and thrown them out of balance.

That is what has occurred in connection with the increased menace of the black widow spider. Man-made structures have shielded the spider from the elements and preying creatures of the wild, and thus she has propagated to such an extent that her presence has taken on the aspects of a plague. Even more important is the fact that mankind—somewhere along the line—has hindered the propagation of the natural enemy of the black widow, whether it be reptile, mammal, arachnid, or insect. It is of foremost importance that we discover this natural enemy and do everything possible to encourage its increase. And if one is to be enabled to decide the identity of this spider's nemesis, he must keep in mind the fact that the creature should have a taste only for black widows, must be capable of multiple propagation, and must be of nation-wide distribution.

Many wild speculations have been advanced as to the identity of this will-o'-the-wisp. In one instance (during the later part of 1934) the newspapers tagged the solpugid. This is a spider-like creature with eight spine-covered legs and, if a male, a segmented, torpedo-shaped abdomen; if a female, a balloon-shaped body. It is as large as a tarantula, yellow in color, sports a hairy covering, and presents a most formidable appearance. The solpugid is not equipped with poison glands but is armed with powerful claws. The claws have been known to infect human beings with whom they came in contact.

This creature's method of procuring food is interesting. When hunting—because of its hairy appearance and great speed—the creature resembles a tuft of thistledown blown before the wind. Upon reaching the hunting-ground the solpugid halts in its headlong course and sniffs about the locality, for all the world like a bloodhound on the scent. The strange creature is not limited to the horizontal plane but climbs trees and fences with great proficiency. After sighting a prospective insect morsel, the creature stalks it in the most orthodox fashion—and at a snail's pace—until within striking distance. Then, with a lightning-like movement, it traverses the intervening space, striking down and capturing its quarry.

These qualifications could well identify the solpugid as the natural enemy of the black widow spider were it not for two interesting facts. The first is that the solpugid does not have a particular liking for *Latrodectus mactans*, and when pitted against her, does not always emerge the victor. This has been learned only after repeated testings in the laboratory. In tilts of solpugid versus black widow, the victories and defeats—over a long period of trials— were held even. Thus if we were to reason as have the solpugid's proponents, we could equally proclaim that the black widow is the natural enemy of solpugid. Another reason why the solpugid falls short of this special classification is that the genus' scope is local, its habitat being limited to the warm areas of the South and Southwest.

These findings of ours had, in 1934, a special significance. This was due to the fact that the press bolstered its contention for this "natural enemy" of the black widow spider by citing as their authority a woman professor of biology in a southern California university. When our laboratory conclusions differed from the alleged statement of the professor in question, we proceeded to get in touch with her. Questioned, she stated emphatically that she had not given out a statement for the press, had neither been interviewed in person nor telephoned by the reporters, and first knew of the article when reading it in the evening papers. "In fact," she said, "they must have consulted a university catalog in order to ascertain my name and position." It was thus that the solpugid arose overnight and was summarily disposed of as a potential natural enemy of the black widow spider. It was never mentioned again.

Bufo marinus, a species of toad, has also been put forward as the black widow's natural enemy. The only objection is the simple fact of its being a toad. Let us consider this robust toad. This creature, in order to deplete the black widow spider population, would have to perform such unbufonoid acts as squeezing into cracks beneath boards and stones, crawling up the studding in garages and homes, creeping through dense shrubs and hedges, and leaping nimbly into the air and picking spiders from the centers of their webs. In actual performance, however, this toad must limit its services to seizing upon those black widow spiders caught wandering upon the surface of the earth. And, since such wanderers would be few and far between, *Bufo marinus* cannot be seriously considered as the natural enemy of the black widow spider.

In this connection, serious attention has also been turned toward the San Diegan alligator lizard, *Gerrhonotus multicarinatus webbii*. Cowles experimented with it at length. In 1931 he discovered that the grounds about his home were infested with black widow spiders. To rid his premises of the dangerous creatures, he cast about to discover their natural enemy, and as a probability, considered the San Diegan alligator lizard. He found that in the laboratory *Gerrhonotus* not only devoured the matured female black widow spider, but went further and gobbled up the eggs, sac and all. The fact that this lizard usually attacks only moving objects made this action seem significant. Cowles decided to experiment further.

So from the laboratory he took *Gerrhonotus*, and loosed several individuals of the species about the garden and within the vicinity of the garage. This structure was, he discovered, the principal hideaway of the spider. He maintained a close surveillance, and by January of 1937 was able to report an abundant increase in lizards. He repeatedly observed them climbing about the interior of the garage, sometimes as high as eight feet from the ground. Occasionally, when closing the garage, he noted that specimens were caught between the lintel and the top of the doors. But the one significant fact noted was that the increase of *Gerrhonotus* corresponded with the decrease in *Latrodectus*.

Conclusive evidence that the lizard had a hand in the latter condition was, however, totally lacking. Because the black widow has no bones or hard body substances, the stomach contents of the lizard failed to afford any clues. Then, too, there was the added difficulty of being unable to detect the lizard—under natural conditions—invading the spider's web. Hence at best there was only circumstantial evidence that *Gerrhonotus* played a dominating role in ridding the premises of the black widow spider.

Unluckily, too, the lizard cannot thrive except under certain conditions, some of which would be obnoxious to householders. These conditions, however, were met in full by Cowles, an experimenter who was willing to sacrifice personal convenience in order to attain knowledge. They are, first, a willingness to harbor a multitude of snake-like, slithering creatures; second, corresponding indifference to untidy and slovenly premises, a condition necessary to the maintenance of such an army of reptiles. Finally, the house cat must be eliminated, since *Gerrhonotus* is a preferred delicacy of the feline family. In short, this lizard must be restricted either to the laboratory or to select locations of comparatively small area wherein these conditions have been met.

Other proposed predators upon the black widow spider which fall short in at least one—and in some instances all—of the fundamental essentials of the creature's natural enemy include the vireo, pigeon, domestic hen, field mouse and related mammals, and some of the hunting spiders, as well as the vinegarroon and centipede.

There are other creatures, however, which come at least within range of being proved agents of black widow destruction. A small parasitic fly (*Gaurax araneae* Coquillett, *Pseudo-gaurax signata* Loew) has been largely mentioned both in scientific and popular literature. P. H. Timberlake, Associate Entomologist, University of California, in a letter to the authors relates the early history of this insect in its relation to mankind. A. Davidson, M. D., a Los Angeles physician, discovered *Gaurax* during the course of his entomological investigations in the nineties. Soon after, Coquillett named the fly *G. araneae*. The creature then lapsed into obscurity and remained undiscussed until the drought of 1934, when the United States was menaced with a rapid increase of black widow spiders. At this time several entomologists revived the discussion, hailing *Gaurax* as the natural enemy of *L. mactans*. Their contention was based upon the fact that the fly has been known to deposit her eggs upon the surface of the spider's egg sac, where after an interval of two or three days they hatch, the tiny larvae worming themselves through the fabric and into the cocoon. Once inside, they feed upon the young spiders and eggs, following which—under this favorable condition—pupation takes place. Weeks pass; the fly-cocoons develop and burst; and by moving through the sac the *G. araneae* emerge into the open air, there to start the cycle all over again.

Herms, Bailey, and McIvor have described other likely black widow parasites. They refer particularly to a dipterous fly of the family *Chloropidae*—found in various sections of California—which enters the cocoon and feeds upon the contents. These students also described a wasplike parasite of the genus *Gelis*, which, like the above, is a predator while in the larval stage. Research and observations in both instances have been conducted in field and laboratory.

Still another parasite, *Baeus californicus* Pierce, has been mentioned as a natural enemy of the black widow. Pierce and associates found the tiny creature—a wasp belonging to the family *Scelionidae*—in sand dunes near Playa del Rey, in close proximity to Los Angeles, during the autumn of 1938. A related species, *B. latrodecti* Dozier, had seven years previously been discovered in Haiti. *Baeus* has been described as a tiny creature, only the male being provided with wings. The female is possessed of a pair of extended legs which enable her to leap at least two inches, a distance more than sixty-five times her own length. After cutting her way into the cocoon the creature oviposits separately in each egg; hence a single larva destroys but a single egg. Despite this painstaking, individual attack, close observations have proved that it is, on the whole, 98.55 per cent effective.

More than a score other species of parasites have been found in spider egg sacs, and these have been reared in the laboratory. Success attended a portion of the experiments, but not to the degree that any particular species could be singled out as the predator of black widow spider eggs.

Our own observations covering a period of several years have been concerned with the mud-dauber wasp. We have found that the various species, including *Chalybion cyaneum*, which has a special taste for black widow spiders, prefer the immature specimens as food for their unhatched young. The wasp searches out the nest of the black widow and springs upon its victim, paralyzing the creature with its stinger. It then grasps the stunned spider with its forelegs and wings its way homeward, which abode is usually situated under the eaves of a human habitation, or attached to the ceiling of a porch, garage, or outhouse, and is composed of many cells arranged somewhat like a honeycomb. The morsel is tucked away tightly into one of the earthen cells, after which the busy wasp flies away upon another similar foraging expedition. The process is continued until the cell has been filled with black widows, upon which the provident mother deposits an egg and carefully seals the tiny room with clay. She then directs her attention to another cell and repeats the process. As each wasp is hatched, it turns immediately to the well-stocked larder. It eats much and grows rapidly, shortly passing through that state of inactivity which transforms it into a winged insect ready to bag a full quota of black widows for its forthcoming brood.

It is obvious that the most destructive enemy of any certain species of wildlife is that one which strikes at the root of life, that is, the elimination of the adult progenitors of the species in question. The destroying of potential spiders—the eggs—is merely a slight setback to the promulgation of the species, since the mother, if unharmed, will immediately set about the task of producing another brood.

Enemies of the black widow spider should be encouraged to propagate and multiply. Those parasitic insects which prey upon *L. mactans* should be permitted to roam unhampered in their outdoor habitats, and increasing efforts must be made to evaluate their spider-destroying propensities. The mud-dauber's nest, heretofore considered only as an evidence of untidiness, may now be accepted as indicative of human enlightenment, the abode of a known destroyer of the world's most poisonous arachnid.

An appalling record of human suffering has been double-checked back to *Latrodectus mactans* and her prototypes. There is no appeal from the indictment, and mankind must now make a unified effort toward curtailment of the greatest arachnid menace the world has ever known.

APPENDICES

Unpublished Medical Reports

∿∿∿

A FURTHER source of data concerning black widow spider bite and its effects upon man consists of an extensive correspondence with physicans, registered nurses, and lay heads of hospitals. This we early realized, and such communications have resulted in our being provided with not only a numerical listing of case histories, but, in many instances, the full details of same. A few of these reports have had prior publication and these are included here only because they have since been augmented by additional information. The letters also revealed a surprising degree of concurrence in observations regarding the symptoms in human beings resulting from the bite of *Latrodectus mactans*, as well as the various conditions under which the culprit is encountered, together with the biological habits of the spider. This is all the more significant in that these reports are made up of findings from independent investigations.

From the state of New Jersey, W. Malcolm McLeod, Superintendent of the Elizabeth General Hospital and Dispensary in the city of that name, tells of a case admitted to that institution which ended in death. The patient, a male, was forty-three years of age, in good health, an American, white; his occupation was engineering. The professional diagnosis was an "infected insect bite of the left leg (probably spider), overwhelming toxic poisoning of the whole body (not septic), acute diffuse peritonitis, pulmonary edema, cellutitis of the leg (left) and thigh, erysipelas of the skin of the abdomen, and acute myocarditis." The patient entered the hospital several days after the first symptoms appeared and died on the seventh day following admission.

From Virginia, there are five communications. Lewis E. Jarrett, M. D., Director of the Medical College of Virginia, Hospital Division, Richmond, reports thirty-two cases of black widow spider bite. W. Carey Henderson, M. D., Nassawadox, speaks of having personally treated five or six cases, and further states that in his community fellow physicians have, over a fifteen-year period, reported fifteen others. C. B. Morton, M. D., of the University Hospital, Charlottesville, states that at that institution there are "as many as three to six cases a year, and quite possibly more than that. . . ." W. Lowndes Peple, M. D., of the McGuire Clinic, St. Lukes Hospital, Richmond, writes of having seen two or three cases. Judson T. Vaughan, M. D., of Ashland, states that he and his associate, Edwin D. Vaughan, M. D., have treated approximately sixty cases over a period of ten years. He informs us that 90 per cent of the black widow spider bites originated in privies. The affected part was, in a majority of instances, either the penis or buttock.

From West Virginia, we have two communications. F. C. Hodges, M. D., of Huntington, reports four cases. J. Bankhead, M. D., of the Charleston General Hospital, tells of having received information from "a very good authority" concerning one death from the bite of a black widow spider, and of having personal knowledge regarding three non-fatal cases. The fatal instance was in a male child two years of age. The tot was walking barefooted in the garden late in the afternoon with his grandparents, when he complained of something sticking him on the great toe of one foot. Immediately following the complaint he became stricken with cramps and vomiting, was carried into the house, and died within the hour before medical assistance could be obtained. Subsequent examination of the toe revealed a puncture wound and, when the grandfather searched the vicinity where the attack had occurred, he found a black widow spider on the underside of a loose flagstone in the walk.

From Tennessee we received five communications. J. M. Dorris, M. D., of Memphis, reports an annual average of one or two cases treated at the Baptist Hospital. Joe B. Wright, M. D., of Lynville, reports four cases of black widow spider bite. Barney Brooks, M. D., who is connected with Vanderbilt University Hospital, Nashville, incorporated his cases with those of Henry T. Kirby-Smith, M. D., of the Emerald-Hodgson Hospital of Sewanee. In private practice, Kirby-Smith witnessed nine cases over a period of five years and the records at the Vanderbilt University Hospital, which he reviewed, show fifteen additional cases over a fourteen year period. In the total series of twenty-four cases "there was one fatality, this being a sixty-nine-year-old white man who was bitten one morning and died late that night." Lon C. Johnson, M. D., of Woodstock, writes of having treated black widow spider-bite cases within recent years. Seventy-five per cent of his patients were, so he states, bitten on the genitals.

We have two communications from Kentucky. Morris H. Thompson, M. D., of Louisville, reported three cases, and tells of another which was originally diagnosed as perforated peptic ulcer. In the latter case upon the patient being questioned, a history of spider bite on the toe was revealed, the spurious diagnosis was corrected, and an unnatural operation avoided. Hart Hagan, M. D., of Fulton, lists seven cases.

From South Carolina, we have the report of Norman O. Eaddy, M. D., of Sumter, who mentions four cases of spider bite, "all of which developed excruciating abdominal and chest pains."

Three communications were received from North Carolina. W. C. Bostic, Jr., M. D., of Forest City, refers specifically to four cases and also states that he has witnessed over a three-year period an annual average of six to ten cases of arachnidism. Joseph J. Combs, M. D., of Raleigh reports a case. A. M. Cornwell, M. D., of the Gordon Crowell Memorial Hospital, Lincolnton, lists three cases of spider bite treated at that institution, and three additional cases which resulted in death. The first fatality, aged forty-eight and in good health, was bitten on the scrotum by a black widow spider while he was sitting on the threshold of a barn door. A physician was called within half an hour and the symptoms noted were a burning, itching sensation in the scrotum, abdominal pain, backache, nausea, fever, chills, extensive swelling of scrotum and abdominal wall, and, by the third day, much suppuration. The patient "died on the seventh day with an extensive erysipelas of the scrotum, hips and abdomen." The second fatality, a male about fifty years of age, was bitten on the right thigh. After three days of severe illness he died, his case having been aggravated by an acute nephritis that developed soon after the spider bite. "The patient had a previous history of recurrent attacks of nephritis." The third fatality was not Dr. Cornwell's case. It was a child, in good health, who "developed no complications as far as the history could be obtained."

From Georgia, we have five communications. J. A. Shields, M. D., of Lafayette, states that he has treated a total number of six cases of black widow spider bite. Eugene R. Corson, M. D., of Savannah, mentions that four or five cases have come under his observation, in one of which the patient, an adult male, "was thrown into convulsions and was able to get up only after three weeks of suffering and loss of flesh." J. A. Redfearn, M. D., of Albany, refers to a case he observed. H. M. Tolleson, M. D., of Eastman, reports a case; and W. A. Walker, M. D., of Cairo, mentions eleven cases treated by himself. In Walker's cases, one patient, a woman fifty-five years of age, writhed and screamed in pain, and in another, a young man who was bitten about sunset while engaged in thrashing peanuts, the victim could be heard moaning two blocks distant.

Concerning cases in Alabama, Maurice J. Abrams, M. D., of Brewton, reports ten, and Groesbeck Walsh, M. D., of the Employees Hospital, Fairfield, states that the Employees Hospital has had about sixty cases of black widow spider bite. Walsh writes that "black widow spider bite has been better known and better understood by the laity, I think, than by the profession." He also relates the history of a case which was unique in several respects. The patient was a young Negro woman, in excellent health and of a strong build. She got up in the morning, chopped some wood, visited a privy, ate breakfast, and became ill about an hour afterward. The symptoms were intense abdominal pain, generalized abdominal muscular rigidity and some evidence of mental disturbance. Eventual collapse and death occurred at about five o'clock that afternoon. The illness was at first diagnosed as having been caused by the eating of potted meat products, and thus became the grounds for a suit at law. Walsh sat in the court as an advisor to the defendant but did not consider the spider angle until the suit was decided. He now believes, however, that she "died of the bite of a black widow spider received either in the wood yard or in the privy."

From Florida, Jean Kennedy, R. N., of Jacksonville, lists three cases which her father, the late George D. Kennedy, M. D., witnessed. She also mentions two other cases which occurred in the locality where she resides. James T. Pate, General Superintendent of Duval County Hospital, also at Jacksonville, lists eight cases wherein the patients may have been—although it could not be stated definitely—victims of black widow spider bite. Henry E. Palmer, M. D., of Tallahassee, writes that he has treated more than fifty cases, and has collected facts concerning twenty authentic cases of spider poison treated by other physicians within a radius of fifty miles of his home city. He declares it to be "the most horrible suffering" he has ever witnessed excepting that resulting from tetanus.

W. H. Browning, M. D., of Shreveport, Louisiana, tells of reports from reliable physicians concerning eleven cases within the vicinity of that city and of having personally witnessed three or four. Roy C. Young, M. D., of Covington, reports attending one case with Frank F. Young, M. D., and consultation in two cases.

Nathan B. Lewis, M. D., former chief surgeon of the Mississippi State Charity Hospital at Vicksburg, states that over an approximate period of five years, there were thirteen cases of black widow spider bite at the institution with which he was then connected.

J. B. Ellis, M. D., of Helena, Arkansas, speaks of having personally treated twenty-five cases.

K. H. Aynesworth, M. D., of Waco, Texas, in one year saw and reported several cases. W. Howard Wells, M. D., also of Waco, writes of a personal acquaintance with seven cases of black widow spider bite. One case "developed anuria for a period of thirty-six hours and almost died, being swollen over the face and the entire body." Paul Gallagher, M. D., of El Paso, speaks of having treated a probable dozen cases and of having seen in consultation a half dozen others. "In one instance, the patient, a tall and muscular woman weighing about 180 pounds who resided on a ranch, developed a paralysis of both legs about 40 minutes after a bite on the upper arm, and this before she had suffered any pain whatsoever." A. H. Voss, M. D., of Odem, reports sixteen cases. One, a sixty-nine-year-old man, died eight weeks after the bite. He believes, however, that death was due to coronary thrombosis.

Zenas B. Noon, M. D., of Nogales, and W. L. Minear, M. D., of Patagonia, Arizona, in collaboration report seventeen cases with one fatality, and Minear reports an additional death in which black widow spider bite may have been a contributing factor. In one case, that of a man over seventy, pain was the dominant feature, and measures had to be taken to prevent him from committing suicide. The fatality was that of a child one and one-half years old (case of J. S. Gonzales of Nogales). The baby was bitten on the right index finger, and the symptoms included abdominal pains, vomiting, convulsions, and unconsciousness. The patient regained consciousness but died two days after the bite.

A. D. Vail, M. D., of Springfield, Missouri, reports five cases, two of which were his own and three, referred. Recovery was uneventful. Vere Harlan Routt, R. N., Superintendent of Daviess County Hospital, Washington, Indiana, writes concerning two cases that were admitted to the institution with which she is connected, one of whom died. Helen G. Martin, Superintendent of the Ohio Valley Hospital, Steubenville, Ohio, mentions a black widow spider case treated there.

Irving S. Cutter, M. D., Dean of Northwestern University Medical School, Chicago, declares that "the most vicious thing we have in the way of an insect is the black widow spider. Its venom is not so different from that of the cobra. . . ." D. J. Lewis, M. D., of Chicago, states that he has•treated four cases of black widow spider bite. Tom Kirkwood, M. D., of Lawrenceville, Illinois, reviews four cases. In addition to these, he has knowledge of several other people having been bitten within his vicinity.

C. P. Bryant, M. D., of Seattle, Washington, writes of having witnessed the effects of black widow spider poison on a patient, a male seventy-four years of age, who was bitten in the region of the left temple. He ultimately recovered, but had "great anxiety to the extent of fear of impending death."

A. A. Soulé, M. D., of Klamath Falls, Oregon, reports two deaths from the bite of the black widow spider. One was that of "a little girl," who said that a "big black bee stung her." There was evidence of severe abdominal pain and mild delirium, and the respiration was embarrassed. The patient died after seven days of suffering. The other case was that of a female twenty years of age, a potato picker, who was "bitten while sleeping in an old granary." She had severe abdominal pain which resembled appendicitis, and also hysteria. "She soon developed encephalitis and died 3 or 4 days following the bite."

California provides numerous medical reports. Emerson C. Savage, M. D., of Keene, mentions having observed one case of black widow spider bite. Russell M. Gray, M. D., of Palm Springs, had approximately one hundred black widow spider bite patients over a period of twelve years. Earl H. Coleman, M. D., Medical adviser of Fresno State College, Fresno, treated two spider-bite cases, and Clarence E. Rees, M. D., of San Diego, cared for three cases. P. Berman, M. D., reports 141 patients treated for spider bites at the Los Angeles County Hospital during 1928–1941, which, with Bogen's report in 1926 of fifteen cases, totals 156 cases. Emelyn Eckblad, Medical Record Librarian at the Presbyterian Hospital, Hollywood, reports a case treated by Joseph J. Hilton, M. D.; and Millie Christenson, R. N., reports a case treated by J. H. Marks, M. D., at the Methodist Hospital of Southern California, Los Angeles.

Frederick Proescher, M. D., pathologist of the County of Santa Clara Hospital, San Jose, lists ten cases at that institution over a period of six years. Oliver M. Moore, M. D., of Bell, had "approximately one dozen" black widow spider-bite cases. O. C. Railsback, M. D., writes that at the Woodland Clinic Hospital, Woodland, there have been thirty-nine cases of spider bite over an eleven-year period, thirty-three of which were diagnosed as the work of the black widow spider. The remaining six were classified merely as "arachnoidism," as the spider culprits were not positively identified. The clinical picture in each case was, nevertheless, that of *L. mactans*. In this series of black widow spider bites death occurred to "a man in his seventies who was afflicted with advanced heart disease. . . ." H. M. Ginsburg, M. D., lists ninety-six cases of black widow poisoning treated prior to 1937 at the General Hospital of Fresno County at Fresno, of which he is director, and an additional fifty or sixty cases treated there between 1937 and 1940.

Charles Barton, M. D., Assistant City Health Officer, Los Angeles, lists two cases, one of which concerns himself. He recorded his own symptoms and administered treatment. Included among the symptoms was amnesia. Elliott P. Smart, Medical Superintendent of Bret Harte Sanatorium, Murphys, cared for three victims of spider bites. Charline Hardacre, R. N., Record Librarian of Riverside Community Hospital, Riverside, lists six cases as having been treated at that institution over an approximate six-year period.

John C. King, M. D., of Pasadena, states that he has treated at least a dozen cases. The majority of his patients were women who had been bitten on the vulva. The symptoms were severe pain which radiated from the seat of the bite down both legs and thence up the back and abdomen. Nervousness was a prominent symptom and the patient usually became "hysterical." One patient, an adult male, was in a hospital for a number of months, and another, an adult tubercular male, died.

From the reports listed above, all advanced by professional practitioners or reliable heads of hospital institutions, several significant conclusions are presented. The first of these provides an indication of the extent to which man has suffered through the agency of the black widow spider. A total of 1,008 cases have been reviewed with fourteen deaths, several of which have been reported in detail. Sixty-three official communications to the authors from twenty-two states have been cited. Only in those instances where a definite figure was specified, or when a certain number of cases per year was mentioned, were the cases tabulated. In instances wherein the correspondent told of his having, for example, treated "four or five cases," the lesser number has been cited. In other instances not quoted herein, letters were received in which statements were made that the writers "had heard" or "read in the papers," of deaths from bites of the black widow spiders. While each source may have stated an authentic fact, we could not, because of insufficient information and the lack of a thorough check, include such material in our data.

We point out, as a second important consideration, the fact that the reports cover the Atlantic seaboard states, the Gulf states, the Great Lakes states, and the Pacific coast states, as well as the states intervening. Our investigations have thus indicated that no section of the country is free from the presence of the black widow spider.

Finally, a sober recapitulation of the foregoing will

establish the fact that this creature is in its relation to mankind the author of dreadful suffering. The expression used (or suggested) in several instances, "almost died," is of great import to the intelligent person, as is the symptom picture. The bite of *Latrodectus mactans* thus should be classified as an ever-present and even deadly possibility.

Lay Histories

~~~~~~

ADDITIONAL evidence may be obtained from experiences of persons who have been bitten by black widow spiders. The newspapers have from season to season featured the most unusual cases of black widow spider bite. Accordingly, to determine the truth of the accounts and also to be able to present the spider-bite theme from all viewpoints, including laymen's reports, we conducted an investigation. In so doing, we in some instances corresponded with the actual victims. At other times we took notes from verbal statements made to us. In cases where the patients were minors, we secured statements from the parents; and, concerning those victims deceased because of the spider bite, information was obtained from their near relatives.

Our questionnaire was lengthy. We asked for the year, the month, the day, and the hour in which the patient experienced the bite, and his location at that precise moment. We also inquired as to the victim's immediate reactions when bitten. Other queries included: Did you note the spider, and where did it come from? Upon what portion of the body were you bitten? Describe the pains you experienced at successive stages. How long an interval elapsed between the time you were bitten and the arrival of the doctor? What was your age at the time of being bitten? Your state of health?

We received fifteen responses. Two of the cases headlined in the newspapers as fatalities resulting from spider bite were reported by our correspondents as erroneous, death having resulted from other causes. This suggests the possibility of other newspaper-announced spider-bite fatalities as misinformation. Three instances diagnosed as spider bite also proved in error, as the recorded symptom picture seemed obviously not that of arachnidism. Ten of the cases, however, were probably due to black widow spider bite, and three of these resulted in deaths.

We shall first review the seven non-fatal cases. The patients were a four-year-old boy who was bitten on the right arm while playing on the lawn; a thirty-three-year-old former registered nurse (female) who experienced the bite on the underside of the right forearm while in a garage looking over some old books; an eleven-year-old girl who received the bite under the left arm pit while assisting her mother in the kitchen; a sixty-year-old retired publisher who was attacked by a black widow spider while he was sleeping; a twenty-three-year-old welder who was bitten just above the right elbow while searching for a tool in the shop; a twenty-seven-year-old housewife who felt the bite on the index finger of the right hand; and a twenty-two-year-old farm hand who was bitten just above the left ankle. The bites occurred before dawn, in the afternoon, evening, and at night. The spider was captured and identified as the black widow spider in six of the seven cases. The symptoms included pains in the abdomen, legs, chest, back, and arms, and also vomiting, perspiration, weakness, muscle spasms, and dizziness. Other symptoms described differed from those more commonly observed, and they may have represented individual types of reaction. Still other recorded symptoms were those not to be expected from spider poisoning, and may have been the sequelae of unwise treatment. Certain mentioned symptoms that were atypical might, perhaps, have been owing to faulty description by the observers.

Herewith are reports of the three fatal cases, which, owing to their significance, are told in detail. The first case concerns W. E., a physician, whose experience was told us by his widow. At 6:00 A.M. on May 20, 1934, the victim, aged fifty-five and in "very good health," felt the bite of the black widow spider. The creature, of unusually large size, came from beneath the seat of a privy and bit him three times on the right groin and testicle. Fiery, excruciating pain followed, and the abdominal wall subsequently became rigid to the extent that the muscles became as stiff as a board. The victim, being a physician, diagnosed his own case and decided upon the treatment of same. Antiseptics and narcotics were powerless to relieve the pain. He therefore decided to use only hot medicated applications, together with internal potions of alkaline liquids.

Four days after receiving the bite, however, he suffered a stroke of paralysis, which affected his speech and caused his whole right side to become "totally paralyzed." He was then taken to the hospital. Following the stroke, a total loss of appetite ensued, which symptom endured several weeks. Owing to his inability to swallow, the patient was fed intravenously over a period of two weeks.

An unsuspected complication then developed in the

form of a diseased appendix. Because of the absence of feeling on his right side due to the paralysis, the patient "was unable to diagnose his case until the appendix ruptured and the pain moved to the left side." In April, 1935, almost a year following the bite of the spider, he died "from the effects of peritonitis after an operation for a ruptured appendix, which he, himself, indicated to the surgeon. . . ."

The next fatal case concerns Mrs. E. O., sixty years of age and in "fairly good health," who was bitten by a black widow spider at 6:00 A.M. on September 3, 1938. The incident occurred in an outdoor toilet, and the spider, a matured black widow, came from beneath the seat. The patient was bitten on the fleshy part of the hip. Excruciating pain followed almost immediately, and continued to such an extent that within an hour after the bite the woman developed hysteria.

The physician, who arrived about that time, gave her a medicine to be taken internally. This had little effect. About an hour later, the suffering becoming so intense, he was compelled to resort to hypodermics. On the afternoon of the fourth day, with no abatement in the pain, the physician advised that she be hospitalized. Accordingly, the patient entered the hospital at 4:00 P.M. on the same day.

The suffering of the woman continued. From the moment of the bite there was a loss of appetite, and for a period of more than seven days she refused food, although the attendants in charge did attempt to feed her intravenously. The most prominent symptom was the pain, the patient declaring that "it seemed that someone was tearing her toe nails off, or burning her feet with a hot iron. . . ." The pain grew steadily worse, and when the effects from the hypodermic began to wear off, she would become delirious. She died September 10, at 10:00 A.M.

The third case which ended in death concerns a young man, W. L., the circumstances of which were communicated to us by his mother. He was twenty-one years of age, unmarried, did not use alcohol and "was never sick a day in his life." His height was five feet, eleven inches, and he weighed 180 pounds. On the morning of September 10, 1938, he lay sound asleep on a screened porch of his parent's home. At 4:00 A.M. sharp pain at the point of his elbow aroused him from sleep, upon which he called his mother, who examined the place at which the pain was indicated. The mother was unable, with the naked eye, to locate a wound of any kind, notwithstanding which, both surmised that some creature had either bitten or stung him. She looked carefully about the premises, and tore the bed apart examining each crack and crevice. The only evidence of insect life to be found was the presence on the porch of a yellow jacket. Some ordinary liniment was obtained and rubbed into the skin of the elbow, after which he again fell asleep. The following morning as he left for work, his mother asked him about the sore arm, upon which he replied: "O. K., only a little stiff when I bend it."

By nine o'clock, however, he became "sick at the stomach and was sore all over to the touch." He left his work and returned home. At eleven o'clock, seven hours after he had been bitten, he, with his mother, visited a physician who immediately diagnosed the case as black widow spider bite. By that time the patient's temperature had risen to 103 degrees, and he felt "sick and weak." The doctor administered a preparation to stimulate the heart and relieve the pain, and as additional treatment told him to stay in bed, drink all the liquid that he could hold, but to eat no solid food. By the fourth day his temperature was up to 105 degrees, but on the following day it again dropped to normal. At this time, however, his arm started to swell and continued to do so. That night the physician, who waited upon the patient in company with a consultant, informed the mother that the worst was over and that "he will be all right."

The mother nevertheless had her son removed to the hospital. She was aware of his intense suffering and the condition of his arm—which by that time was swollen along its entire length—and believed that he would be more comfortable there and, obviously, could more readily obtain medical services should there be a relapse. A further examination at the hospital revealed that the patient's heart and lungs were in excellent condition, and with this as a basis, an opinion was rendered that recovery would take place. Despite this prediction, W. L. died September 17, seven days after the bite.

These case histories possess value in that they reveal the usual weaknesses to be found in lay reports and also, despite this, convey factual data. It was recognized from the beginning that much of the information transmitted would lack professional accuracy. Accordingly, we were not surprised to find the accounts far from complete or reliable, inasmuch as the observers were not often capable of distinguishing the effects of the bite from extraneous factors. Perhaps it is just this indiscriminate and mixed clinical data that, in part, delayed recognition of the truth concerning spider bite. The communicated case histories, nevertheless, exemplify the intense interest that many laymen manifest towards arachnidism.

The fatal cases necessitate an appraisal. W. E., the physician, very likely had his hemiplegia as a result of the spider bite, since the rise in blood pressure usually noted after the bite might plausibly be expected to cause such an accident. The later consequences of the cerebral hemorrhage, paralysis, suffering, appendicitis, and peritonitis were then—in this case—only remotely and indirectly related to the spider bite. The case of Mrs. E. O., the sixty-year-old female, suggests similarities with that of the above, and may have been mediated by a cerebral lesion, as indicated by the delirium, refusal to eat, etc. Unfortunately, sufficient medical data is not given here to evaluate her case. W. L., the twenty-one-year-old son, appears to have been a typical case of arachnidism, but complicated by an infection, probably streptococcic in nature, with a consequent fatal septicemia. The time sequence of the symptoms here is characteristic of the development of secondary infection following the bite. The fact should not be overlooked, however, that in each case the spider bite initiated the condition that terminated in death.

APPENDIX III

Tables

wwwwwwwwwwwwwwwwwwwwwwwwwwwwwwwwwwwwwwwwwwwwwwwwwwwwwwwwwwwww

1. NUMBER OF REFERENCES TO SPIDER BITES BY YEARS

Years	Number
B.C.	6
1 A.D. to 500 A.D.	6
500 to 1000	3
1001 to 1500	10
1501 to 1750	66
1751 to 1800	25
1801 to 1850	74
1851 to 1875	93
1876 to 1880	25
1881 to 1885	63
1886 to 1890	54
1891 to 1895	50
1896 to 1900	24
1901 to 1905	56
1906 to 1910	52
1911 to 1915	50
1916 to 1920	49
1921 to 1925	73
1926 to 1930	136
1931 to 1933	75
1934 to 1936	165
1937 to 1940	132
1941 to 1943 (Aug.)	383
	1670

2. TABLE OF REPORTED SPIDER BITES BY STATES—1726 TO 1943

State	Reports	Cases	Deaths
Alabama	8	71	1
Arizona	4	18	2
Arkansas	3	31	0
California	41	578	32
Colorado	5	2	0
Connecticut	2	0	0
Delaware	1	0	0
Florida	8	126	0
Georgia	14	37	0
Idaho	2	4	2
Illinois	6	17	2
Indiana	2	2	1
Iowa	2	0	0
Kansas	5	3	1
Kentucky	3	12	0
Louisiana	6	33	0
Maine	1	0	0
Maryland	2	2	0
Massachusetts	2	2	0
Michigan	2	0	0
Minnesota	1	0	0
Mississippi	2	13	0
Missouri	2	5	0
Montana	2	0	0
Nebraska	2	1	0
Nevada	1	0	0
New Hampshire	1	0	0
New Jersey	1	1	1

TABLE OF REPORTED SPIDER BITES BY STATES
1726 TO 1943 (cont.)

State	Reports	Cases	Deaths
New Mexico	2	0	0
New York	3	3	0
North Carolina	9	34	3
North Dakota	1	0	0
Ohio	3	3	1
Oklahoma	3	4	1
Oregon	3	2	2
Pennsylvania	3	3	1
Rhode Island	2	1	0
South Carolina	2	4	0
South Dakota	1	0	0
Tennessee	7	34	1
Texas	13	61	2
Utah	1	0	0
Vermont	1	0	0
Virginia	14	173	1
Washington	3	2	0
West Virginia	3	9	1
Wisconsin	1	0	0
Wyoming	1	0	0
Total............	207 reports	1291 cases	55 deaths

Black widow spider reported
in 48 states. Cases in 32
states. Deaths in 17 states.

SOURCES

1. Books and Articles Primarily of Scientific Interest

Amaral, Afranio do. "Specific Antivenins to Combat Scorpionism and Arachnidism," *Bull. Antivenin Inst. America,* II (1928), 69–71.

Baerg, W. J. "The Effects of Bite of *Latrodectus Mactans* Fabr.," *Jour. Parasitology,* IX (1923), 161–69.

———. "Poisons of Scorpions and Spiders and their Effect and Treatment," *Natural History,* XLII (1938), 42.

———. "Regarding the Habits of Tarantulas and the Effects of their Poison," *Scientific Monthly,* XIV (1922), 482–89.

Banks, J. T. "Spider Bite, Severe Symptoms and Unusual Phenomena," *Atlanta M. and S. J.,* VI (1860).

Barton, Charles. "How it Feels to be Bitten by a Black Widow Spider—a Case History," *Natural History,* XLII (1938), 43–44.

Beasley, R. N. "Death from Bite of a Trapdoor Spider," *Med. Jour. Australia,* I (1930), 255.

Blackwall, J. "Experiments and Observations on the Poison of Animals of the Order Araneida," *Trans. of the Linnean Society of London,* II (1855), 31–38.

Blair, A. W. "Life History of Latrodectus Mactans," *Arch. Int. Med.,* LIV (1934), 844–50.

———. "Spider Poisoning. Experimental Study of the Effects of the Female Latrodectus Mactans in Man," *Arch. Int. Med.*, LIV (1934), 831–43.

Blanchard. An article on the House Spider in *Hardwicke's Science Gossip*, II (1866), 202.

Blanchard, A. D. "More Evidence Bearing on Spider Bites" (Correspondence), *Insect Life*, I (1889), 313.

Bogen, Emil. "Arachnidism. Spider Poisoning," *Arch. Int. Med.*, XXXVIII (1926), 623–32. Prize essay of the California Medical Association.

Bogen, Emil, and Loomis, R. N. "Poisoning Poisonous Spiders; Experimental Investigation in Control of Black Widow Spider (*Latrodectus Mactans*)," *Calif. and West. Med.*, XLV (1936), 31–38.

Bordas, L. "Recherches sur l'effet des piqûres du Latrodectus Guttatus ou Malmignatte," *Compt. Rend. Acad. d. Sc.*, CXXXIII (1901), 953–55.

Brazil, V., and Vellard, J. "Contribuição ao estudo do veneno das aranhas; lycosa raptoria, ctenus nigriventer; genero latrodectus. . . ," *Memorias do Instituto de Butanan*, III (1927), 243–99.

Brown, C. W. "Poisonous Spiders of Southern California," *South. Calif. Practitioner*, X (1895), 451.

Brown, W. L. "Spider Bite, Case Report," *Southwestern Med.*, VIII (1924) 131.

Browning, C. C. "Original Investigations of Spider Bites in Southern California," *South. Calif. Practitioner*, XVI (1901), 291–300.

Castelli, A. "Sulla tossicita della punture del Latrodectus tredecimguttatus," *Arch. di Farmacologia Sperimentale*, XVI (1913), 183–92.

Chamberlin, R. V. and Ivie, Wilton. *The Black Widow Spider and its Varieties in the United States*. Bull. Univ. of Utah, Vol. XXV. Salt Lake City, 1935.

Comstock, J. A case of very singular nervous affections, supposed to have been occasioned by the bite of a tarantula, in *Medical Repository of New York*, Vol. I (1803).

Comstock, John Henry. *The Spider Book; a Manual for the Study of the Spiders . . . and other Members of the Class* Arachnida, *found in America North of Mexico. . . .* New York, 1912. Rev. and ed. by W. J. Gertsch, 1940.

Cook, A. J. "The Black or Poisonous Spider," *Calif. Cultivator and Live Stock and Dairy Jour.*, XXIV (1900), 291.

Corson, E. R., "The Spider Bite Question Again" (Correspondence), *Insect Life*, I (1889), 280–82.

Cowles, R. B. "San Diegan Alligator Lizard and the Black Widow Spider," *Science*, N. S., LXXXV (1937), 99–100.

D'Amour, F. E., Becker, F. E., and Van Riper, W. "The Black Widow Spider," *Quar. Rev. of Biol.*, XI (1936).

Davidson, A. "Parasites of Spider Eggs," *Entomological News*, VII (1896), 319–20.

De Asis, C. "Red Back Spider Bite and Magnesium Sulphate Treatment," *Amer. Jour. Trop. Med.*, XIV (1934), 33–44.

"Deaths," *Jour. Am. Med. Assoc.*, LXXXIII (1924), 83. Death of C. W. Caldwell from septicemia following spider bite.

Duges, A. A. "A Spider Bite Contribution" (Correspondence), *Insect Life*, II (1889), 47.

Duffield, A. "A Spider Bite," *New England Med. Gazette*, XXVII (1892), 9.

Eaton, Alvah A. "On the Poisonous Bite of the Spider, *Latrodectus Mactans*" (Correspondence), *Insect Life*, IV (1892), 277.

Emerton, James Harvey. *The Common Spiders of the United States.* Boston and London, 1902.

Escomel, E. "The *Latrodectus mactans* . . . in Peru," *New Orleans M. & S. J.*, LXX (1917), 530.

Ewing, H. E. "Afield with Spiders," *National Geographic Magazine*, LXIV (1933), 163–94.

——. "On Spider Bites," *Amer. Jour. Trop. Med.*, VIII (1928), 39–62.

Fabre, Jean Henri Cassimir. *The Life of a Spider*. Trans. by Teixeira de Mattos. New York, 1913.

——. *Souvenirs entomologiques. Etudes sur l'instinct et les moeurs des insectes.* 10 vols., Paris, 1879–1907. Vols. VIII and IX.

Finlayson, M. H. " 'Knoppie-Spider' Bite," *South African Med. Jour.*, X (1936), 43–45.

——. "Specific Antivene in Treatment of 'Knoppie-Spider' Bite," *South African Med. Jour.*, XI (1937), 163–67.

Frawley, J. M., and Ginsburg, H. M. "The Diagnosis and Treatment of Black Spider Bite," *Jour. Am. Med. Assoc.*, CIV (1935), 1790–92.

Frost, C. "On the Katipo, a Poisonous Spider of New Zealand," *Trans. and Proc. N. Z. Inst.*, II (1869), 81.

Graells, Mariano de la Paz. "Sur les accidents provoqués en catalogue par le Theridion malmignatte," *Annales de la Société Entomologique de France*, Vol. III (1834).

Gray, R. M. "Black Widow Spider Poisoning. Preliminary Report on Bite of . . . *Lactrodectus Mactans*," *Calif. and West. Med.*, XLIII (1935) 328–31.

Grinnel, F. "Poisoning from the Bite of a Spider," *Cincinnati Lancet and Observer*, XIX (1876), 900.

Hall, W. W., and Vogelsang, W. A. "Spider Poisoning; Study of Toxin of Black Spider (*Latrodectus Mactans*)," *U. S. Naval Med. Bull.*, XXX (1932), 471–78.

Hasselt, A. W. M. van. "Het Spinnenvergift," *Nederlandsch Tijdschrift voor Geneeskunde*, XVIII (1882), 57–70.

Hentz, Nicholas M. "Descriptions and Figures of the Araneidas of the United States," *Jour. Bost. Soc. Nat. Hist.*, VI (1850), 271. Reprinted in Hentz's *The Spiders of the United States*, Boston, 1875.

Herms, W. B., Bailey, S. F., and McIvor, Barbara. *The Black Widow Spider*. Univ. of Calif. Coll. of Agric. Bull., No. 591. Berkeley, 1935.

Hodgdon, A. L. "Bite of a Poisonous Spider, *Latrodectus Mactans*," *Jour. Am. Med. Assoc.*, XLVIII (1907), 1506.

Hopton, A. "Poisoning from the Bite of a Spider Successfully Treated," *New York Med. Jour.*, II (1829), 297.

Houssay, B. A. "Contribution à l'étude de l'hemolysine des araignées," *Compt. Rend. Soc. de Biol.*, LXXXIX (1916), 658.

Hulse, I. "Bite of a Spider on the Glans Penis followed by Violent Symptoms; Recovery," *Am. L. M. Sc.*, XXIV (1839), 69–72.

Ingram, W. W., and Musgrave, A. "Spider Bite (Arachnidism). Survey of its Occurrence in Australia, with Case Histories," *Med. Jour. Australia*, II (1933), 10–15.

Kellaway, C. H. "Venom of Latrodectus hasseltii," *Med. Jour. Australia*, I (1930), 41–46.

Kellogg, Vernon L. "Spider Poison," *Jour. Parasitology*, I (1915), 107–12.

Kennedy, George D. "On Spider Bites," *Amer. Jour. Clin. Med.*, XXVIII (1921), 859.

Kobert, Rudolf. *Beiträge zur Kenntnis der Giftspinnen*. Stuttgart, 1901.

Koch, Carl Ludwig. *Die Arachniden. Getreu nach der Natur abgebildet und beschrieben*. Nürnburg. 16 vols., 1831–1848. Vol. VIII.

Larsen, N. P. "The Black Spider," *Mid-Pacific Magazine*, XXXVI (1928), 13.

Lebert. "De l'action veneneuse des araignées sur l'homme," *Bull. Soc. med. dela Suisse Rom.,* IX (1875), 311–18.

Leeuwenhoek, A. van. "Concerning Spiders, their way of Killing their Prey, Spinning their Webs, Generation, etc.," *Philos. Trans. of the Royal Society,* XXII (1702), No. 272, p. 867.

Lethbridge, H. V. Discussion. *Med. Jour. Australia,* II (1929), 486.

Louis, D. J. "Black Spider Poisoning; Report of Four Cases," *Jour. Am. Med. Assoc.,* LXXVI (1921), 99.

Lucas, Pierre Hippolyte. *Histoire naturelle des crustacés, des arachnides et des myriapodes.* Paris, 1840.

McCook, H. C. *American Spiders and their Spinning Work.* 3 vols., Philadelphia, 1889–1893. Vol. I.

McKay, W. J. S. "Red-backed Spider Bite," *Med. Jour. Australia,* March, 1928, p. 322.

McKeown, Keith C. *Spider Wonders of Australia.* Sydney, 1936.

Marmocchi, F. "Memoria sopra il Ragnorosse dell' Agro Volterrano," *Atti dell' Accad. d. Sc. di Siena,* VIII (1800), 218–23.

Martin William. *The New Zealand Nature Book.* 2 vols., London, 1930. Vol. I.

Mazza, S. "Contribucion al Estudio del Aracnoidismo," *Rev. de la San. Mil.* Buenos Aires, 1910.

Meek, J. M. Correspondence in *Hardwicke's Science Gossip,* XIII (1877), 46.

Moore, W. "A Tarantula Case," *Homeopathic Recorder,* Lancaster, XVIII (1903), 9.

Musgrave, A. "Harmful Australian Spiders," *Australian Museum Mag.,* III (1927), 134.

Peck, E. D. "Poisoning from Snake and Spider Bites," *Medical Progress,* VII (1896), 386.

Petrunkewitch, A. I. "Latrodectus, the Poisonous Spider," *Scientific American,* C (1909), 395.

Pickard-Cambridge, F. O. Arachnida, Araneida. Biologia Centrali Americana. 2 vols., 1889–1905.

Pierce, William D. "The Black Widow Spider and Parasites," Bull. South. Calif. Acad. Sci., Vol. XXXVII (1938).

Presley, R. E. "A Case of Spider Bite," Memphis Medical Monthly, XVI (1896), 520–22.

Reese, Albert M. "Venomous Spiders," Science, N. S., LIV (1921), 382–85.

Riddick, T. M. "A Case of Poisoning from the Bite of a Black Spider," North Carolina Med. Jour. XLI (1897), 247–49.

Riley, C. V., and Howard, L. O., "A Contribution to the Literature of Fatal Spider Bites," Insect Life, I (1889), 204–11.

Robie, Thomas. "On the Effects of . . . the Venom of Spiders," Philos. Trans. of the Royal Society, XXXIII (1724), 20–22.

Rodway, F. A. "The Red-backed Spider" (Correspondence), Med. Jour. Australia, I (1927), 770.

Rulison, E. T. Discussion in Calif. and West. Med., XXXIII (1925), 873.

Sachs, H. "Zur Kenntnis der Kreuzspinnengiftes," Beiträge zur chemischen Physiologie und Pathologie: Zeitschrift für die gesamte Biochemie, II (1902), 125–33.

Savory, Theodore H. The Biology of Spiders. New York, 1928.

———. British Spiders: Their Haunts and Habits. Oxford, 1926.

Schenck, A. H. "Spider Bites," Texas Med. Jour., XII (1896), 493.

Semple, G. W. "Cases of Spider Bite," Virginia Med. Monthly, II (1875), 633–38.

Serrao, Franc. "Lezione academiche de Francisco Sarrao" (1742, Napoli), trans. (*De vita et scriptis Francisci Serai*), by Vicq-D'Azyr, Naples, 1784.

Sharp, E. L. "Poisonous Bites and Stings," *Medical Progress*, XX (1904), 358.

Shipley, A. E. "Crustacea and Arachnids," *Cambridge Natural History* (London, 1909), VI, 362.

Simon, Eugene. "Note sur le mico, l'araignée venimeuse de Bolivie," *Compt. Rend. Soc. Ent. de Belgique*, Vol. CLXX (1886).

Skaife, S. H. *Animal Life in South Africa.* Cape Town, 1920.

Smith, E. E. "Another Spider Bite" (Correspondence), *Insect Life*, III (1891), 392.

Smithers, R. H. N. "Notes on Distribution of Knoopie-spinnekop (*Latrodectus Indistinctus*), South Africa *Med. Jour.*, XIII (1939), 33–34.

Squibb, E. R. and Sons. Antivenin Circular, 1936.

Stahl, D. "Bite of a Spider, succeeded by Alarming Symptoms," *Am. J. M. Sc.*, XXII (1838), 514.

Taylor, Charlotte. "Spiders, their Structure and Habits," *Harper's Mag.*, XXI (1860), 461–77; XXII (1861), 323.

Thompson, D. S. "Supposed Spider Bite, Severe Symptoms, Rigidity of the Muscles, Prostration, etc.," *N. and S. Reporter*, V (1860), 111.

Tompkins, H. H. "Spider Bite with Severe Symptoms," *Med. Bull.* VI (1884), 207.

Toti, L. "Memoria sopra il Falangio o Ragno Veneficio dell' Argo Volteranno," *Atti dell' Accad. d. Sc. di Siena*, VII (1794), 244–65.

Troise, E. "Preparación de un suero inmumizante contra el Latrodectus mactans," *Rev. Soc. Argent. de Biol.*, IV (1928), 467–75.

Turpin, T. J. "Black Spider Poisoning" (Correspondence), *Jour. Am. Med. Assoc.*, LXXVI (1921), 54.

Tuttle, George W. "Making a Living out of Insects," *Outing*, LXXIX (1921), 75–76.

Vellard, J. *Araignées venimeuses de Bresil.* Comm. Conf. Panamericaine d'Hygiene Buenos-Aires, 1934.

———. [Estudio de los animales venenosos], *Gac. Méd. de Caracas*, XLIII (1936), 53, 68, 85, & 105.

———. *Le Venin des Araignées.* Paris, 1936.

Wade, W. L. "Spider Bites," *South. Calif. Practitioner*, IV (1889), 344.

Walckenaer, Charles Athanase, and Gervais, Paul. *Histoire naturell des Insectes. Aptéres.* Librairie Encyclopedique de Roret. 4 vols., Paris, 1837–1847. Vols. I and IV.

Warburton, Cecil. *Spiders.* Cambridge and New York, 1912.

Watson, J. R. "The Bite of Latrodectus mactans" (Correspondence), *Science*, N. S., LV (1922), 539.

Wight, R. Allan. "The New Zealand Katipo," *Insect Life*, II (1889), 134.

———. "The Spider-Bite Question," *Insect Life*, I (1889), 348.

Wilder, B. G. "Experiments with Spiders," *Harper's Mag.*, XXXIV (1866), 450.

Wilson, J. T. "Poisoning by the Bite of the Southern Spider," *Trans. South. Surg. and Gynec. Assoc.*, V (1893), 406–11.

Woody, W. S. "Spider Bite of the Glans Penis Stimulating an Acute Abdominal Condition," *New York Med. Jour.*, CXV (1922), 542–43.

Worcester, O. E. "Spider Bite," *Alkaloid Clin. Chicago*, X (1903), 1191.

Wright, F. W. "On the Katipo, a Poisonous Spider of New Zealand," *Dominion Med. Jour.*, II (1869), 202.

Wright, W. G. "On Spider-bite Cases," *Insect Life*, II (1889), 46.

2. Books and Articles containing References and Allusions to Spider Lore and Legend

Abbott, Charles C. *Recent Rambles, or, In Touch with Nature.* Philadelphia, 1892.

Ball, James Dyer. *Things Chinese, or Notes connected with China.* London, 1926.

Brewer, E. C. *Dictionary of Phrase and Fable.* London and Philadelphia, 1905.

Brewer, W. H. *Up and Down California, 1860–1864,* New Haven, 1930.

Butler, Samuel (1612–1680). "On a Hypocritical Nonconformist," in works posthumously published, 1715–1717. On the subtle spider.

Coolidge, Dane, and Mary R. *The Navajo Indians,* New York, 1930.

[Cornelio, Thomas]. "Extract of a Letter, written March 5, 1672, by Dr. Thomas Cornelio . . . concerning some Observations made by Persons Pretending to be Stung by Tarantulas," *Philos. Trans. Royal Soc.,* VII (1672), No. 83, p. 4066.

Curtis, Natalie. *The Indian Book.* New York and London, 1907.

De Beck, B. Bunky and the "Black Widow Spider Woman." Comic Strip, King Features Syndicate, 1936.

Diogenes, Laertius (418–323 B.C.). *The Lives and Opinions of Eminent Philosophers.* Trans. by C. D. Yonge, London, 1901.

Emans, Elaine V. *About Spiders: Introducing Arachne.* New York, 1940.

Fabricius, Johan Christian. *Systema Entomologiae Sistens Insectorum, Classes, Ordines, Genera, Species, etc.* 1775.

Gifford, E. W., and Block, Gwendoline H. *California Indian Nights Entertainments.* Glendale, Calif., 1930.

Goldsmith, Oliver. *An History of the Earth and Animated Nature,* 4 vols., Philadelphia, 1795. Vol. IV.

Hall, James. *Notes on the Western States.* Philadelphia, 1838.

Hecker, J. F. C. *The Epidemics of the Middle Ages.* Trans. by B. G. Babington, London, 1844. Part II: On the Dancing Mania.

Howitt, Mary. *The Spider and the Fly.* 1821.

Hudson, W. H. *The Naturalist in La Plata.* London, 1892.

James, Robert. *A Medicinal Dictionary, including Physic, Surgery, Anatomy, Chymestry, and Botany in all their Branches relative to Medicine.* 3 vols., London, 1743–1745. Vol. I.

The Koran. Trans. from the Arabic by J. M. Rodwel. London and New York, 1909.

Lankester, Sir Edwin Ray. *Great and Small Things.* London, 1923.

Lloyd, J. T. "Spiders used in Medicine," *Electic Medical Journal,* Dec., 1920; also in *Amer. Jour. Pharmacy,* XCIII (1921), 18–24.

Mackie, R. L. *The Story of King Robert the Bruce,* New York, 1913.

Manly, W. L. *Death Valley in '49.* San Jose, Calif., 1894.

Mead, Richard. *Mechanical Account of Poisons.* London, 1702.

Merriam, C. Hart. *The Dawn of the World. Myths and Wierd Tales Told by the Mewan Indians of California.* Cleveland, Ohio, 1910.

"The Natural History of the Tarantula," *Once a Week,* XXIX (1873), 567.

Ovid [Publius Ovidius Naso]. *Metamorphoses,* Book VI.

Pepys, Samuel. *Diary.* 9 vols. New York, 1893–1899. Entry for Feb. 4, 1662.

Pliny [Plineus Secundus Caius]. *The Natural History of Pliny.* Trans. by John Bostock and H. T. Riley. London and New York, 1890.

Podolsky, Edward. "Music's Role in Healing," *Etude*, LI (1933), 422.

Polo, Marco. *The Travels of Marco Polo.* Trans. by Marsden, rev. and ed. by Manuel Komroff. New York, 1926.

Pouchett, Felix Archiméde. *The Universe; the Infinitely Great and the Infinitely Little.* New York, 1873.

Puckett, N. N. *Folk Beliefs of the Southern Negro.* Chapel Hill, 1926.

Sanborn, Kate. *A Truthful Woman in Southern California.* New York, 1893.

Segar, E. C. Advice concerning Black Widow Spider. Pop-eye's Cartoon Club, King Features Syndicate. 1935.

Shakespeare, William. "Midsummer Night's Dream," in *Works*, Boston, 1906.

Smith, Peter. *The Indian Doctor's Dispensatory. Being Father Smith's Advice respecting Diseases and their Cure.* Cincinnati, Ohio, 1812; reproduced, 1901.

Southey, Robert. "To a Spider," in *Minor Poems*, 1797–1799.

Spenser, Edmund. "Muiopotmos," in *Complaints*, 1592.

"Tarantism and the Dancing Mania," *Scientific American*, LXXXII (1916), 195.

Thomas, Daniel L. and Lucy B. *Kentucky Superstitions*, Princeton, 1920.

Thorndyke, Lynn. *A History of Magic and Experimental Science*, 6 vols. New York, 1923–1941. Vols. III and IV.

Walckenaer, C. A. Archives litteraires de Vanderburg. Lettre sur la tarantula. 1830.

Werner, E. T. C. *Myths and Legends of China.* London, 1922.

Westen, H. "The Dance of Death," *Photo-Facts,* I (1938), 92–96.

Wood, John George. *The Illustrated Natural History.* London, 1863.

3. Specific Allusions and References *

Abbott. Quoted by Walckenaer and Gervaise, *Histoire Naturell;* cited in *Insect Life,* I, 204.

Albertus Magnus (Fifteenth century). Cited by Thorndyke, *History of Magic.* Tells of child eating spiders.

Antonius, Pius (86–161 A.D.). Cited by Lloyd in *Electic Medical Journal.* On use of spiders for medicinal purposes.

Aristotle (384–322 B.C.). Cited by Vellard in *Le Venin des Araignées.* On use of spiders for medicinal purposes.

Baghlivi, G. (1695). Cited by Lebert, in *Bull. Soc. Med. dela Suisse Rom.*

Bertkau, P. Cited by van Hasselt in *Nederlandsch Tijdschrift.*

Breeger. Quoted from *Scientific American* (Nov. 17, 1888), p. 310.

Burette. Cited by Podolsky in the *Etude.*

Coleman, E. H. Quoted by Kellogg in *Jour. Parasitology.* Reports Coleman's case and experiments.

Cross, J. C. Cited by Banks in *Atlanta M. and S. J.*

Diodorus Siculus (First century B.C.). Cited by McCook in *American Spiders.*

Dick. Quoted by Riley and Howard in *Insect Life.*

Dioscorides, Pedanic (c. 50 A.D.). Cited by Lloyd in *Electic Medical Journal.*

---

* Works cited in this section will be found with complete bibliographical data in sections 1 and 2 of this bibliography.

Dufour. Cited by Fabre in *Souvenirs Entomologiques*, Vol. VIII.

Dumerit. Cited by Pouchett in *The Universe*.

Emerson, R. W. Cited by Brewer in *Dictionary of Phase and Fable*.

Erker. Cited by van Hasselt in *Nederlandsch Tijdschrift*.

Flacourt. Cited by Shipley in *Cambridge Natural History*, Vol. VI.

Frost, C. Cited in *Insect Life*, III, 425.

Gallagher. Cited by Brown in *Southwestern Med.*, VIII.

Geraldy, H. G. (1317). Cited by Thorndyke, *History of Magic*, III. On his being accused of attempting the Pope's life by poison—ashes of spider.

Heinzel. Cited by van Hasselt in *Nederlandsch Tijdschrift*.

Jaeger. Cited by D'Amour, *et al.* in *Quar. Rev. of Biol.*

Legends of Irish wood and of parish roof free from spiders (1008 A.D.). Cited by Savory in *British Spiders*.

Magis Universalis Naturae et Artis (no date). Cited by Podolsky in the *Etude*.

Overbury, Thomas (1581–1613). Cited by Whibley, 1913. On mention of venomous spiders in examination into his murder.

Perotti, N. (1430–1480). Cited by Hecker in *Epidemics of the Middle Ages*.

Strabo (First century A.D.). Cited by McCook in *American Spiders*.

Swift, Jonathan (1666–1745). Cited by Emans in *About Spiders*.

Talmud. Legend of King David and the spider. Cited by Ginsburg, 1909.

Trallianus (Sixth century). Cited by Lloyd in *Electic Medical Journal*. On medicinal use of spiders.

4. Personal Comments

Abrams, M. J. May 12, 1942

Aynesworth, K. H. March 29, 1940

Banks, J. B. September 4, 1941

Barton, C. September 16, 1937

Berman, P. January 10, 1940; June 2, 1942

Blair, A. W. October 15, 1941

Bogen, E. January 15, 1940; February 20, 1942

Bostic, W. C., Jr. June 4, 1940

Brooks, B. March 27, 1940

Browning, W. H. May 17, 1940

Bryant, C. P. August 16, 1941

Christenson, Millie. May 12, 1942

Coleman, E. H. May 31, 1940

Combs, J. J. April, 1940

Cornwell, A. M. January 23, 1940

Corson, E. R. May 11, 1940

Cutter, T. S. March 8, 1940

Dorris, J. M. May 14, 1942

Eaddy, N. O. May 21, 1940

Eckblad, Emelyn. May 12, 1942

Ellis, J. B. March 20, 1940

Fattig, P. W. 1935

Gallagher, P. May 10, 1940

Ginsburg, H. M. March 21, 1940

Gray, R. M. March 26, 1940

Hagan, Hart. May 11, 1942

Hardacre, Charline. August 21, 1941

Henderson, W. C. April 3, 1940

Hodges, F. C. May 18, 1942

Jarrett, L. E. April 20, 1941

Johnson, L. C. May 24, 1940

Jones, D. L. May 12, 1942

Kennedy, Jean. April 25, 1940

King, J. C. March 22, 1940

Kirby-Smith, H. T. April 19, 1940

Kirkwood, T. April 3, 1940

Lake, G. B. May 13, 1942

Lewis, N. B. September 11, 1941

Louis, D. J. May 18, 1940

MacLeod, W. M. October 21, 1941

Martin, Helen G. August 12, 1941

Minear, W. L. May 10, 1942

Moore, O. M. May 28, 1940

Morton, C. B. April 25, 1940

Noon, Z. B. May 16, 1942

Palmer, H. E. April 4, 1940

Pate, J. T. August 8, 1941

Peple, W. L. May 13, 1940

Proescher, F. September 8, 1941

Railsback, O. C. August 4, August 8, 1941

Redfearn, J. A. May 12, 1940

Rees, C. E. June 13, 1940

Routt, Vere Harlan. August 10, 1941

Shield, J. A. May 24, 1940

Smart, E. P. May 8, 1940

Soulé, A. A. May 31, 1940

Thompson, H. M. May 22, 1940

Thompson, R. May 15, 1942

Timberlake, P. H. January 12, 1940

Tolleson, H. M. May 7, 1940

Vail, A. D. May 12, 1942

Vaughan, J. T. January 14, 1940

Villiers, C. de. (To E. Bogen) November 24, 1935

Voss, A. H. May 14, 1942

Walker, W. A. May 18, 1940

Walsh, G. March 23, 1940

Wells, W. H. April 25, 1940

Wilcox, J. M. December 20, 1939

Wright, J. B. May 6, 1940

Young, R. C. May 16, 1942

Index

Ireland, said to have no spiders, 7

Italy, dancing mania in, 14–16; mentioned, 18

Jamaica, spider-bite cases reported from, 55

Jarrett, Lewis E., reports spider-bite cases, 174

Java, tarantulas found in, 23

Jerusalem cricket, as food for black widow spider, 145–46

Jimson-weed, cult of, 10

Jockey spider. *See* Red-back spider

Johnson, Lon C., reports spider-bite cases, 175–76

Kansas, fatal spider-bite case reported from, 64

Karakurt, specimens of placed on breast of man, 41

Katipo, found in New Zealand, 44; home-building sites of, 44; effects from bite of, 45; tests of venom of upon rats, 77

Kennedy, George D., reports spider-bite cases, 63, 178

Kennedy, Jean, reports spider-bite cases, 178

Kentucky, spider-bite cases reported from, 176

Kerosene, to control of black widow spider, 159

King, John C., reports spider-bite cases, 182–83

Kirby-Smith, Henry T., reports spider-bite cases, 175

Kirkwood, Tom, reports spider-bite cases, 180

Knoppie spinnekop. See South Africa

Kolbig convent church, peasants pronounce curse on, 15

Kraken, mythical spider in sea, 6–7

La arana ponzonosa, Mexicans fear, 11

Lachesis jararaca, spider venom tested on, 23

Latrodectus apicallis, black widow spider known as, 126

Latrodectus concinnus, found in South Africa, 42

Latrodectus congoblatus, found in Greece, 39

Latrodectus curacaviensis, found in West Indies, 35

Latrodectus dotatus, black widow spider known as, 126

Latrodectus formidabilis, black widow spider known as, 126

Latrodectus geometricus, description of, 38; in Florida, 34; in California, 34; in West Indies, 35; in South America, 38; in South Africa, 42

Latrodectus hasseltii. See Red-back spider

Latrodectus indistinctus, found in South Africa, 42

Latrodectus intersector, black widow spider known as, 126

Latrodectus karakurt, experiments with, 77

Latrodectus lugubris, bite of, 43

Latrodectus mactans, meaning of, 126; other names for, 126; reported in Hawaiian Islands, 43, 80

Latrodectus perfidus, black widow spider known as, 126

Latrodectus scelio, tests on rats, 77. *See* Red-back spider

Latrodectus tridecimguttatus, found in Italy, 39; experiments with, 77–78

A CATALOGUE OF SELECTED DOVER BOOKS
IN ALL FIELDS OF INTEREST

THE DEVIL'S DICTIONARY, Ambrose Bierce. Barbed, bitter, brilliant witticisms in the form of a dictionary. Best, most ferocious satire America has produced. 145pp. 20487-1 Pa. $1.50

ABSOLUTELY MAD INVENTIONS, A.E. Brown, H.A. Jeffcott. Hilarious, useless, or merely absurd inventions all granted patents by the U.S. Patent Office. Edible tie pin, mechanical hat tipper, etc. 57 illustrations. 125pp. 22596-8 Pa. $1.50

AMERICAN WILD FLOWERS COLORING BOOK, Paul Kennedy. Planned coverage of 48 most important wildflowers, from Rickett's collection; instructive as well as entertaining. Color versions on covers. 48pp. 8¼ x 11. 20095-7 Pa. $1.35

BIRDS OF AMERICA COLORING BOOK, John James Audubon. Rendered for coloring by Paul Kennedy. 46 of Audubon's noted illustrations: red-winged blackbird, cardinal, purple finch, towhee, etc. Original plates reproduced in full color on the covers. 48pp. 8¼ x 11. 23049-X Pa. $1.35

NORTH AMERICAN INDIAN DESIGN COLORING BOOK, Paul Kennedy. The finest examples from Indian masks, beadwork, pottery, etc. — selected and redrawn for coloring (with identifications) by well-known illustrator Paul Kennedy. 48pp. 8¼ x 11. 21125-8 Pa. $1.35

UNIFORMS OF THE AMERICAN REVOLUTION COLORING BOOK, Peter Copeland. 31 lively drawings reproduce whole panorama of military attire; each uniform has complete instructions for accurate coloring. (Not in the Pictorial Archives Series). 64pp. 8¼ x 11. 21850-3 Pa. $1.50

THE WONDERFUL WIZARD OF OZ COLORING BOOK, L. Frank Baum. Color the Yellow Brick Road and much more in 61 drawings adapted from W.W. Denslow's originals, accompanied by abridged version of text. Dorothy, Toto, Oz and the Emerald City. 61 illustrations. 64pp. 8¼ x 11. 20452-9 Pa. $1.50

CUT AND COLOR PAPER MASKS, Michael Grater. Clowns, animals, funny faces . . . simply color them in, cut them out, and put them together, and you have 9 paper masks to play with and enjoy. Complete instructions. Assembled masks shown in full color on the covers. 32pp. 8¼ x 11. 23171-2 Pa. $1.50

STAINED GLASS CHRISTMAS ORNAMENT COLORING BOOK, Carol Belanger Grafton. Brighten your Christmas season with over 100 Christmas ornaments done in a stained glass effect on translucent paper. Color them in and then hang at windows, from lights, anywhere. 32pp. 8¼ x 11. 20707-2 Pa. $1.75

JEWISH GREETING CARDS, Ed Sibbett, Jr. 16 cards to cut and color. Three say "Happy Chanukah," one "Happy New Year," others have no message, show stars of David, Torahs, wine cups, other traditional themes. 16 envelopes. 8¼ x 11.
23225-5 Pa. $2.00

AUBREY BEARDSLEY GREETING CARD BOOK, Aubrey Beardsley. Edited by Theodore Menten. 16 elegant yet inexpensive greeting cards let you combine your own sentiments with subtle Art Nouveau lines. 16 different Aubrey Beardsley designs that you can color or not, as you wish. 16 envelopes. 64pp. 8¼ x 11.
23173-9 Pa. $2.00

RECREATIONS IN THE THEORY OF NUMBERS, Albert Beiler. Number theory, an inexhaustible source of puzzles, recreations, for beginners and advanced. Divisors, perfect numbers. scales of notation, etc. 349pp.
21096-0 Pa. $2.50

AMUSEMENTS IN MATHEMATICS, Henry E. Dudeney. One of largest puzzle collections, based on algebra, arithmetic, permutations, probability, plane figure dissection, properties of numbers, by one of world's foremost puzzlists. Solutions. 450 illustrations. 258pp.
20473-1 Pa. $2.75

MATHEMATICS, MAGIC AND MYSTERY, Martin Gardner. Puzzle editor for Scientific American explains math behind: card tricks, stage mind reading, coin and match tricks, counting out games, geometric dissections. Probability, sets, theory of numbers, clearly explained. Plus more than 400 tricks, guaranteed to work. 135 illustrations. 176pp.
20335-2 Pa. $2.00

BEST MATHEMATICAL PUZZLES OF SAM LOYD, edited by Martin Gardner. Bizarre, original, whimsical puzzles by America's greatest puzzler. From fabulously rare Cyclopedia, including famous 14-15 puzzles, the Horse of a Different Color, 115 more. Elementary math. 150 illustrations. 167pp.
20498-7 Pa. $2.00

MATHEMATICAL PUZZLES FOR BEGINNERS AND ENTHUSIASTS, Geoffrey Mott-Smith. 189 puzzles from easy to difficult involving arithmetic, logic, algebra, properties of digits, probability. Explanation of math behind puzzles. 135 illustrations. 248pp.
20198-8 Pa. $2.00

BIG BOOK OF MAZES AND LABYRINTHS, Walter Shepherd. Classical, solid, and ripple mazes; short path and avoidance labyrinths; more — 50 mazes and labyrinths in all. 12 other figures. Full solutions. 112pp. 8⅛ x 11.
22951-3 Pa. $2.00

COIN GAMES AND PUZZLES, Maxey Brooke. 60 puzzles, games and stunts — from Japan, Korea, Africa and the ancient world, by Dudeney and the other great puzzlers, as well as Maxey Brooke's own creations. Full solutions. 67 illustrations. 94pp.
22893-2 Pa. $1.25

HAND SHADOWS TO BE THROWN UPON THE WALL, Henry Bursill. Wonderful Victorian novelty tells how to make flying birds, dog, goose, deer, and 14 others. 32pp. 6½ x 9¼.
21779-5 Pa. $1.00

DRIED FLOWERS, Sarah Whitlock and Martha Rankin. Concise, clear, practical guide to dehydration, glycerinizing, pressing plant material, and more. Covers use of silica gel. 12 drawings. Originally titled "New Techniques with Dried Flowers." 32pp. 21802-3 Pa. $1.00

ABC OF POULTRY RAISING, J.H. Florea. Poultry expert, editor tells how to raise chickens on home or small business basis. Breeds, feeding, housing, laying, etc. Very concrete, practical. 50 illustrations. 256pp. 23201-8 Pa. $3.00

HOW INDIANS USE WILD PLANTS FOR FOOD, MEDICINE & CRAFTS, Frances Densmore. Smithsonian, Bureau of American Ethnology report presents wealth of material on nearly 200 plants used by Chippewas of Minnesota and Wisconsin. 33 plates plus 122pp. of text. 6¹/8 x 9¼. 23019-8 Pa. $2.50

THE HERBAL OR GENERAL HISTORY OF PLANTS, John Gerard. The 1633 edition revised and enlarged by Thomas Johnson. Containing almost 2850 plant descriptions and 2705 superb illustrations, Gerard's Herbal is a monumental work, the book all modern English herbals are derived from, and the one herbal every serious enthusiast should have in its entirety. Original editions are worth perhaps $750. 1678pp. 8½ x 12¼. 23147-X Clothbd. .$50.00

A MODERN HERBAL, Margaret Grieve. Much the fullest, most exact, most useful compilation of herbal material. Gigantic alphabetical encyclopedia, from aconite to zedoary, gives botanical information, medical properties, folklore, economic uses, and much else. Indispensable to serious reader. 161 illustrations. 888pp. 6½ x 9¼. USO 22798-7, 22799-5 Pa., Two vol. set $10.00

HOW TO KNOW THE FERNS, Frances T. Parsons. Delightful classic. Identification, fern lore, for Eastern and Central U.S.A. Has introduced thousands to interesting life form. 99 illustrations. 215pp. 20740-4 Pa. $2.50

THE MUSHROOM HANDBOOK, Louis C.C. Krieger. Still the best popular handbook. Full descriptions of 259 species, extremely thorough text, habitats, luminescence, poisons, folklore, etc. 32 color plates; 126 other illustrations. 560pp. 21861-9 Pa. $4.50

HOW TO KNOW THE WILD FRUITS, Maude G. Peterson. Classic guide covers nearly 200 trees, shrubs, smaller plants of the U.S. arranged by color of fruit and then by family. Full text provides names, descriptions, edibility, uses. 80 illustrations. 400pp. 22943-2 Pa. $3.00

COMMON WEEDS OF THE UNITED STATES, U.S. Department of Agriculture. Covers 220 important weeds with illustration, maps, botanical information, plant lore for each. Over 225 illustrations. 463pp. 6¹/8 x 9¼. 20504-5 Pa. $4.50

HOW TO KNOW THE WILD FLOWERS, Mrs. William S. Dana. Still best popular book for East and Central USA. Over 500 plants easily identified, with plant lore; arranged according to color and flowering time. 174 plates. 459pp. 20332-8 Pa. $3.50

BUILD YOUR OWN LOW-COST HOME, L.O. Anderson, H.F. Zornig. U.S. Dept. of Agriculture sets of plans, full, detailed, for 11 houses: A-Frame, circular, conventional. Also construction manual. Save hundreds of dollars. 204pp. 11 x 16.
21525-3 Pa. $5.95

HOW TO BUILD A WOOD-FRAME HOUSE, L.O. Anderson. Comprehensive, easy to follow U.S. Government manual: placement, foundations, framing, sheathing, roof, insulation, plaster, finishing — almost everything else. 179 illustrations. 223pp. 7⅞ x 10¾.
22954-8 Pa. $3.50

CONCRETE, MASONRY AND BRICKWORK, U.S. Department of the Army. Practical handbook for the home owner and small builder, manual contains basic principles, techniques, and important background information on construction with concrete, concrete blocks, and brick. 177 figures, 37 tables. 200pp. 6½ x 9¼.
23203-4 Pa. $4.00

THE STANDARD BOOK OF QUILT MAKING AND COLLECTING, Marguerite Ickis. Full information, full-sized patterns for making 46 traditional quilts, also 150 other patterns. Quilted cloths, lamé, satin quilts, etc. 483 illustrations. 273pp. 6⅞ x 9⅝.
20582-7 Pa. $3.50

101 PATCHWORK PATTERNS, Ruby S. McKim. 101 beautiful, immediately useable patterns, full-size, modern and traditional. Also general information, estimating, quilt lore. 124pp. 7⅞ x 10¾.
20773-0 Pa. $2.50

KNIT YOUR OWN NORWEGIAN SWEATERS, Dale Yarn Company. Complete instructions for 50 authentic sweaters, hats, mittens, gloves, caps, etc. Thoroughly modern designs that command high prices in stores. 24 patterns, 24 color photographs. Nearly 100 charts and other illustrations. 58pp. 8⅜ x 11¼.
23031-7 Pa. $2.50

IRON-ON TRANSFER PATTERNS FOR CREWEL AND EMBROIDERY FROM EARLY AMERICAN SOURCES, edited by Rita Weiss. 75 designs, borders, alphabets, from traditional American sources printed on translucent paper in transfer ink. Reuseable. Instructions. Test patterns. 24pp. 8¼ x 11.
23162-3 Pa. $1.50

AMERICAN INDIAN NEEDLEPOINT DESIGNS FOR PILLOWS, BELTS, HANDBAGS AND OTHER PROJECTS, Roslyn Epstein. 37 authentic American Indian designs adapted for modern needlepoint projects. Grid backing makes designs easily transferable to canvas. 48pp. 8¼ x 11.
22973-4 Pa. $1.50

CHARTED FOLK DESIGNS FOR CROSS-STITCH EMBROIDERY, Maria Foris & Andreas Foris. 278 charted folk designs, most in 2 colors, from Danube region: florals, fantastic beasts, geometrics, traditional symbols, more. Border and central patterns. 77pp. 8¼ x 11.
USO 23191-7 Pa. $2.00

Prices subject to change without notice.
Available at your book dealer or write for free catalogue to Dept. GI, Dover Publications, Inc., 180 Varick St., N.Y., N.Y. 10014. Dover publishes more than 150 books each year on science, elementary and advanced mathematics, biology, music, art, literary history, social sciences and other areas.